# Number Word Search

Circle the words in the word search.

```
o a s e v e n t e e n n
n e i g h t e e n b c i
e e n i n e t e e n v n
s i a e l e v e n z a e
e g z t w e l v e z f m
v h g o t o t h e z o o
e t q f i f t e e n q i
n q q t w e n t y a b a
a f o u r t e e n t w o
s i x t e e n t h r e e
s i x t h i r t e e n w
f o u r a f i v e t e n
```

| one | six | eleven | sixteen |
| --- | --- | --- | --- |
| two | seven | twelve | seventeen |
| three | eight | thirteen | eighteen |
| four | nine | fourteen | nineteen |
| five | ten | fifteen | twenty |

# Skip Counting by 2s

Count by 2s.

| | |
|---|---|
| 1. | 44, **46**, ____, ____, ____, ____, ____ |
| 2. | 15, ____, ____, ____, ____, ____, ____ |
| 3. | 82, ____, ____, ____, ____, ____, ____ |
| 4. | 26, ____, ____, ____, ____, ____, ____ |
| 5. | 33, ____, ____, ____, ____, ____, ____ |
| 6. | 50, ____, ____, ____, ____, ____, ____ |
| 7. | 68, ____, ____, ____, ____, ____, ____ |

Count back by 2s.

| | |
|---|---|
| 8. | 30, **28**, ____, ____, ____, ____, ____ |
| 9. | 48, ____, ____, ____, ____, ____, ____ |
| 10. | 64, ____, ____, ____, ____, ____, ____ |

# Skip Counting by 5s

Count by 5s.

| 1. | 0, __5__, ______, ______, ______, ______, ______ |
|----|----------------------------------------------------|
| 2. | 35, ______, ______, ______, ______, ______, ______ |
| 3. | 70, ______, ______, ______, ______, ______, ______ |

Count back by 5s.

| 4. | 50, ______, ______, ______, ______, ______, ______ |
|----|----------------------------------------------------|
| 5. | 35, ______, ______, ______, ______, ______, ______ |
| 6. | 70, ______, ______, ______, ______, ______, ______ |

Circle the groups of 5. Count by 5s and then by 1s.

A B C D E F G H I J K L M N O

P Q R S T U V W X Y Z

______ letters

## Count by 10s

| | |
|---|---|
| 1. | 20, _____, _____, _____, **60**, _____, _____ |
| 2. | 15, _____, _____, _____, _____, _____, _____ |
| 3. | 22, _____, _____, _____, _____, _____, _____ |
| 4. | 43, _____, _____, _____, _____, _____, _____ |
| 5. | 27, _____, _____, _____, _____, _____, _____ |

## Count back by 10s

| | |
|---|---|
| 6. | 100, _____, _____, _____, _____, _____, _____ |
| 7. | 66, _____, _____, _____, _____, _____, _____ |
| 3. | 88, _____, _____, _____, _____, _____, _____ |

# Skip Counting by 5s to 200

Connect the dots counting by 5s to 200.

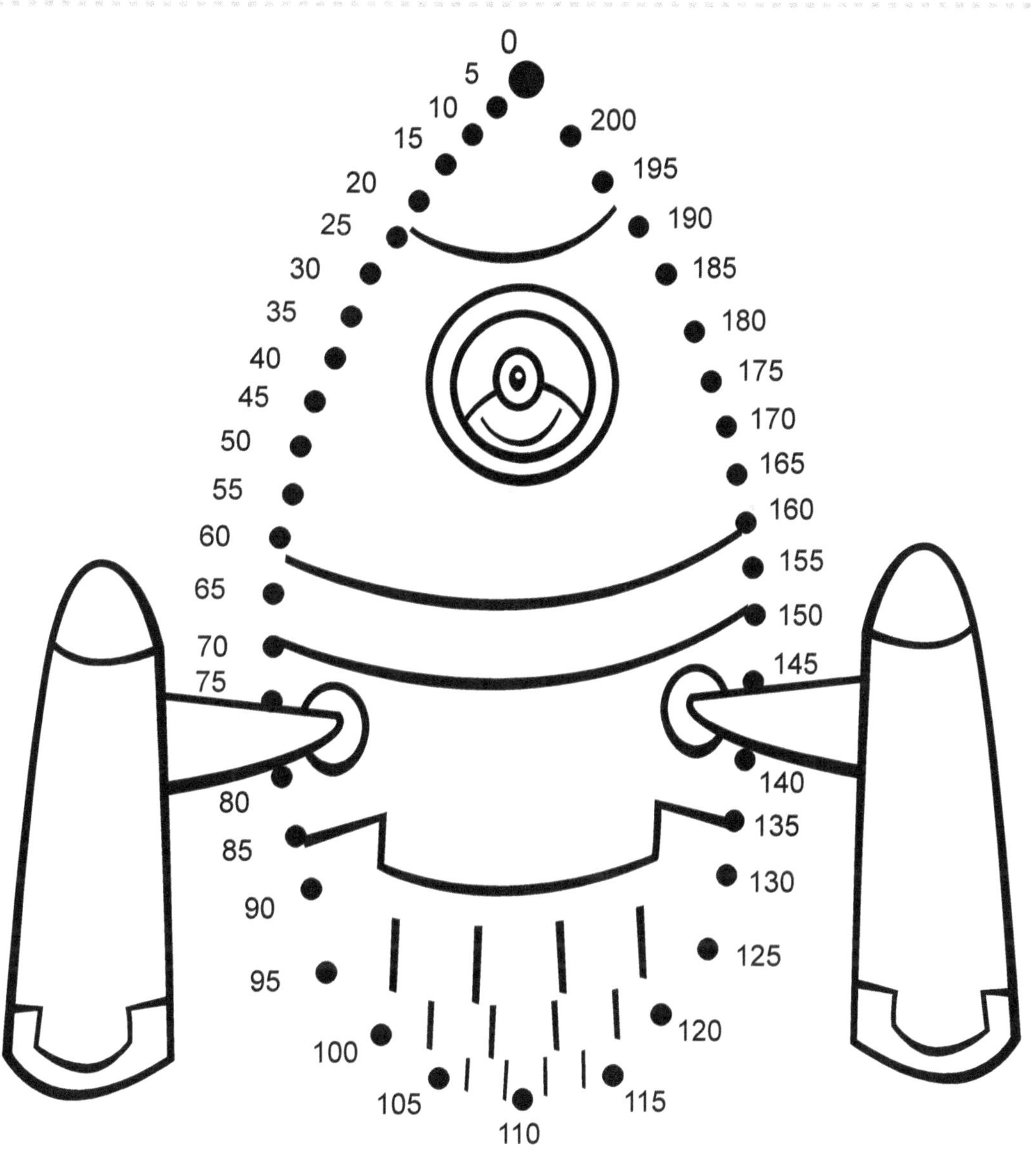


# BRAIN STRETCH

Count back by 5s

100, _____, _____, _____, _____, _____, _____, _____

Count back by 2s

150, _____, _____, _____, _____, _____, _____, _____

# Counting Backward by 1s

Start at 50. Connect the dots counting backward by 1s.

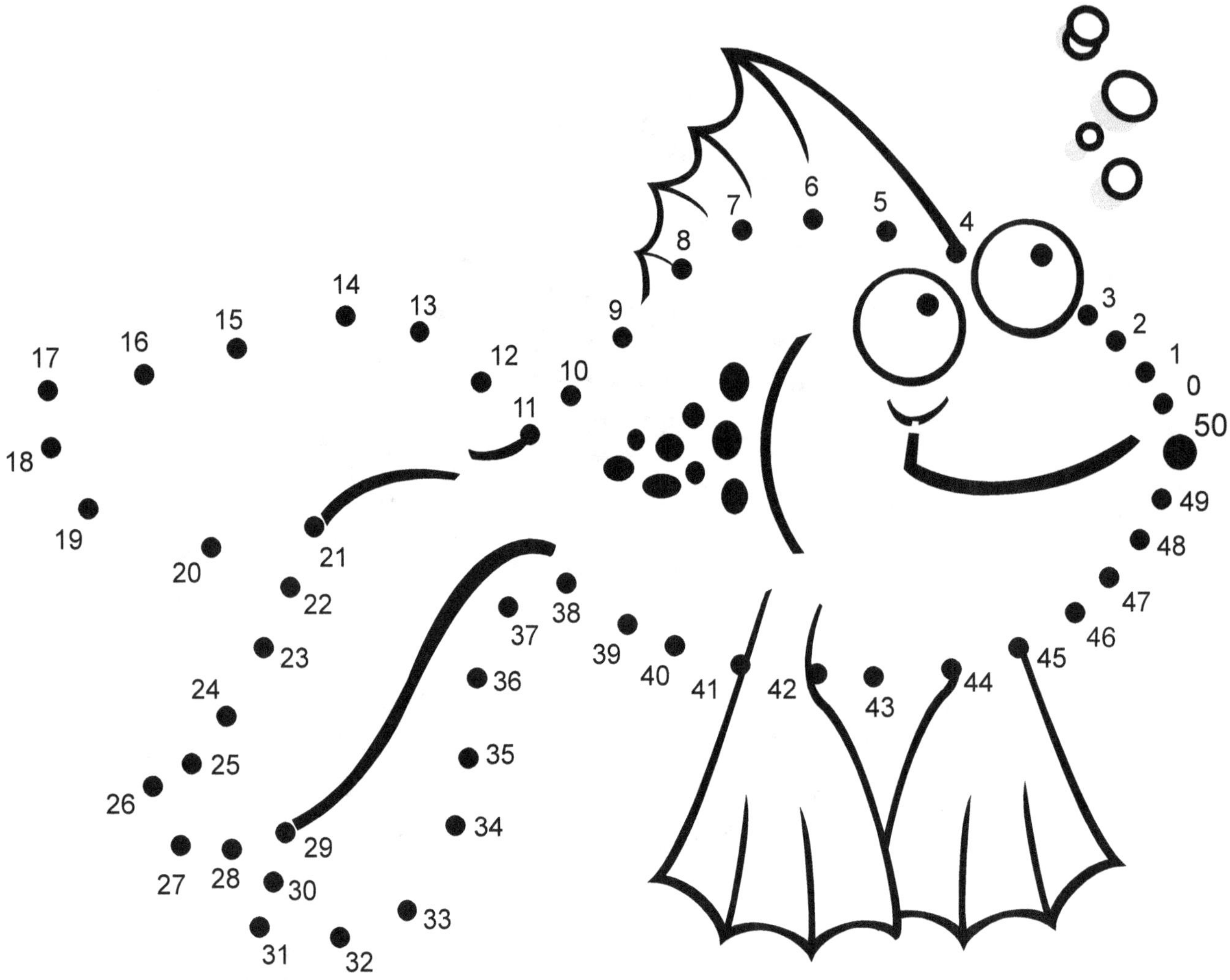

## BRAIN STRETCH

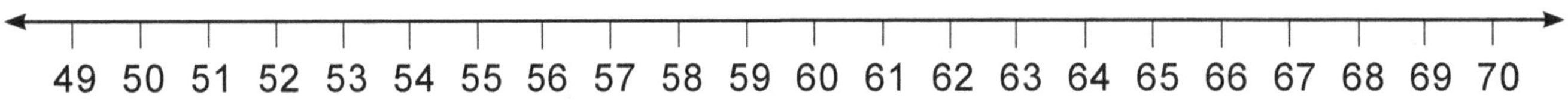

49  50  51  52  53  54  55  56  57  58  59  60  61  62  63  64  65  66  67  68  69  70

What numbers are between 56 and 63? __________________________

What numbers are between 66 and 70? __________________________

# Growing Number Patterns

In a growing pattern, the number increases.

$+2 \quad +2 \quad +2 \quad +2 \quad +2 \quad +2$

2   4   6   8   10   12   14

The pattern rule is add 2 each time.

---

Make a growing pattern by adding.

1. The pattern rule is add 3 each time.

3, ______, ______, ______, ______, ______, ______, ______

2. The pattern rule is add 5 each time.

15, ______, ______, ______, ______, ______, ______, ______

3. The pattern rule is add 10 each time.

5, ______, ______, ______, ______, ______, ______, ______

4. Make your own. The pattern rule is add ______ each time.

6, ______, ______, ______, ______, ______, ______, ______

# Shrinking Number Patterns

In a shrinking pattern, the number decreases.

(−2)    (−2)    (−2)    (−2)    (−2)    (−2)

20    18    16    14    12    10    8

The pattern rule is subtract 2 each time.

Make a shrinking pattern by subtracting.

1. The pattern rule is subtract 3 each time.

27, _______, _______, _______, _______, _______, _______, _______

2. The pattern rule is subtract 5 each time.

35, _______, _______, _______, _______, _______, _______, _______

3. The pattern rule is subtract 10 each time.

100, _______, _______, _______, _______, _______, _______, _______

4. Make your own. The pattern rule is subtract _______ each time.

25, _______, _______, _______, _______, _______, _______, _______

# Odd and Even Numbers

Look at the ones digits to see if a number is odd or even.
Odd numbers end in 1, 3, 5 , 7, or 9.
Even numbers end in 0, 2, 4, 6, or 8.

Color the even numbers orange. Color the odd numbers green.

# Ordering Numbers

1. Fill in the missing numbers.

<table>
<tr><td>Just before: <u>81</u>, 82, 83</td><td>Just before: ____, 65, 66</td></tr>
<tr><td>Just after: 11, 12, ____</td><td>Just before and after: ____, 89, ____</td></tr>
<tr><td>Between: 4, ____, 6</td><td>Just after: 16, 17, ____</td></tr>
<tr><td>Between: 69, ____, 71</td><td>Just before and after: ____, 40, ____</td></tr>
<tr><td>Just after: 33, 34, ____</td><td>Just before: ____, 56, 57</td></tr>
</table>

2. Order each group of numbers from smallest to largest.

54, 29, 71, 18, 27, 11      ____, ____, ____, ____, ____, ____

39, 63, 3, 84, 17, 40      ____, ____, ____, ____, ____, ____

3. Order each group of numbers from largest to smallest.

46, 71, 24      ____, ____, ____          19, 11, 15      ____, ____, ____

# Tens and Ones

Count the tens and ones. Write how many blocks in all.

Each stack has 10 blocks.    Each block is one.

1 ten    +    5 ones    =    15

---

**1.** 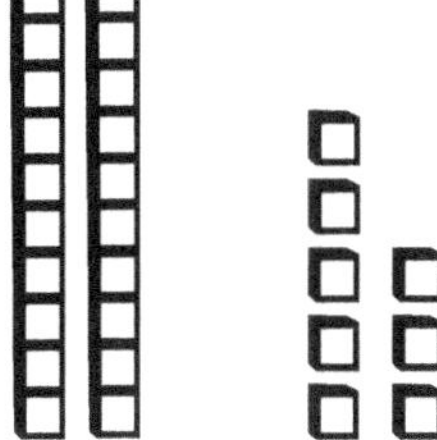

____ tens + ____ ones

Number: ________

**2.** 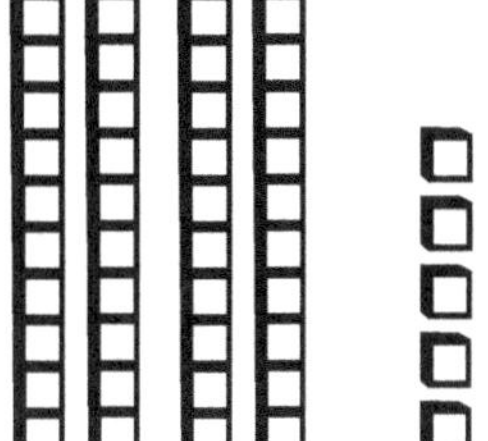

____ tens + ____ ones

Number: ________

**3.** 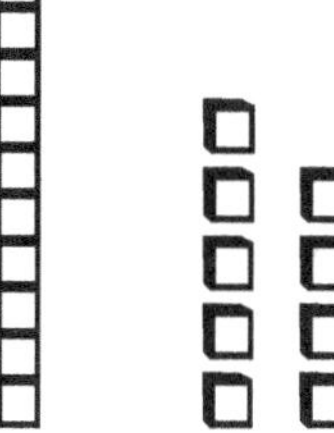

____ tens + ____ ones

Number: ________

**4.** 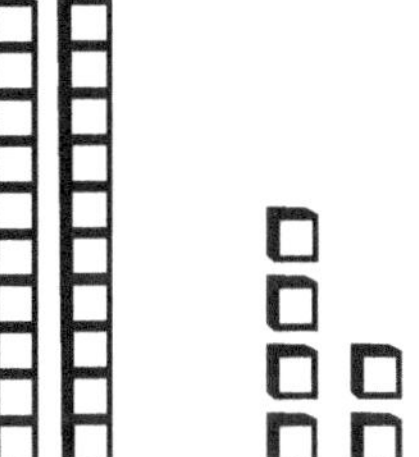

____ tens + ____ ones

Number: ________

**5.** 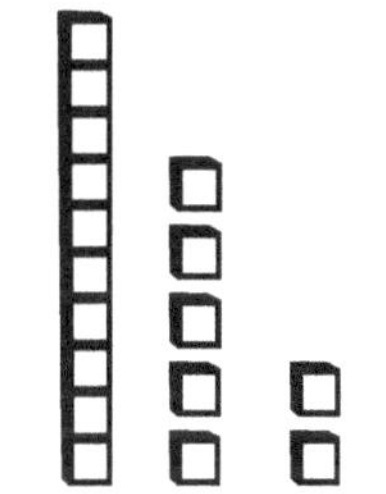

____ tens + ____ ones

Number: ________

**6.** 

____ tens + ____ ones

Number: ________

**7.** 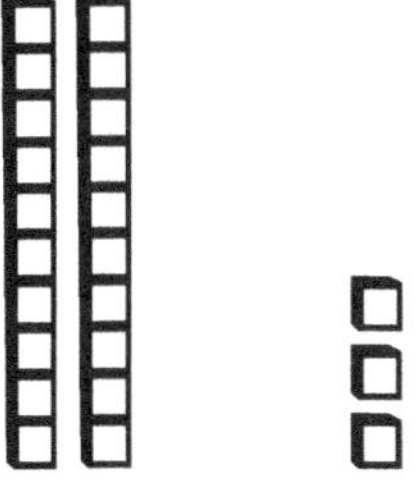

____ tens + ____ ones

Number: ________

**8.** 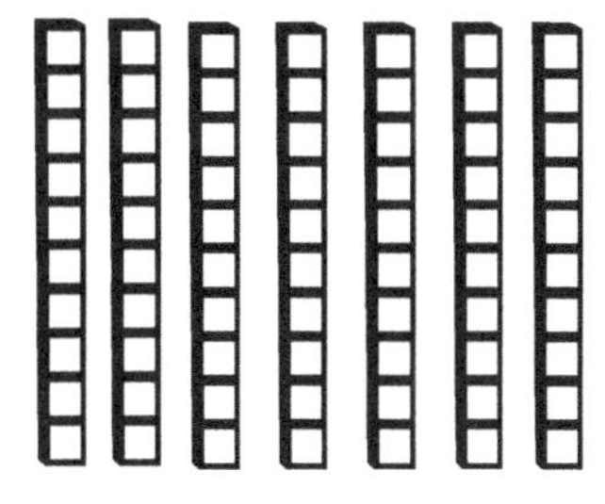

____ tens + ____ ones

Number: ________

**9.** 

____ tens + ____ ones

Number: ________

# Tens and Ones

Count the tens and ones. Write how many blocks in all.

10. 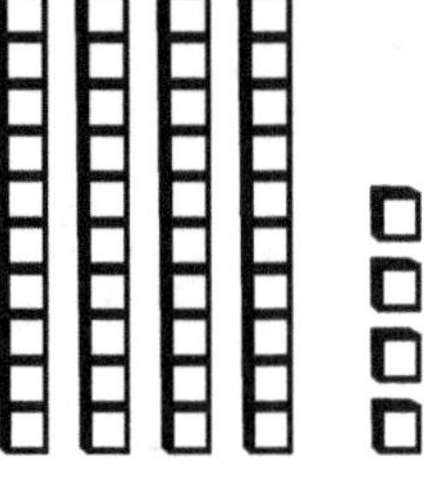

_____ tens + _____ ones

Number: _____________

11. 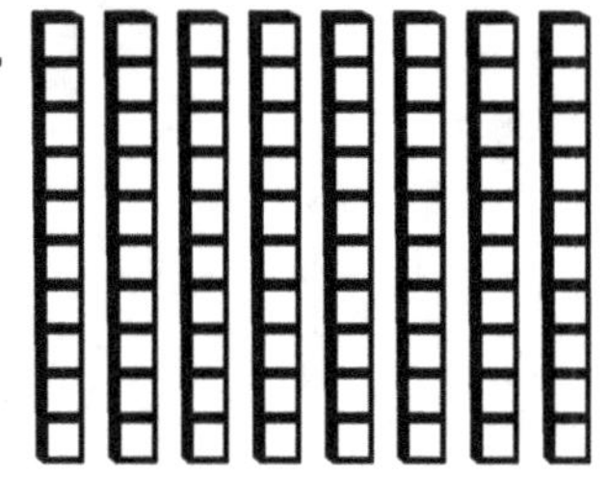

_____ tens + _____ ones

Number: _____________

12. 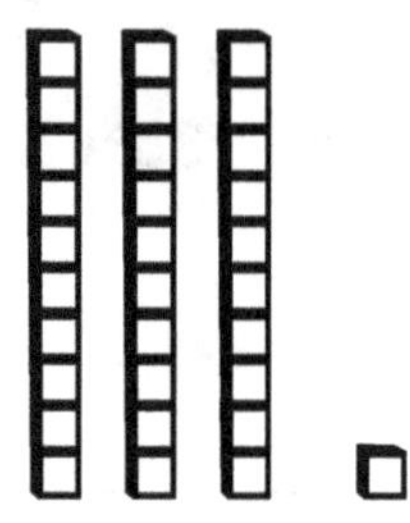

_____ tens + _____ one

Number: _____________

13. 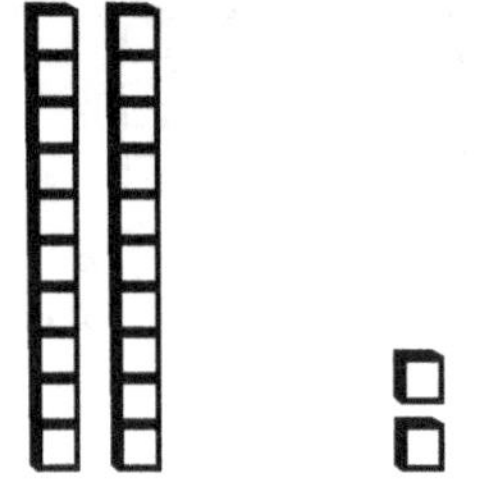

_____ tens + _____ ones

Number: _____________

14. 

_____ tens + _____ ones

Number: _____________

15.

_____ tens + _____ ones

Number: _____________

16.

_____ tens + _____ ones

Number: _____________

17. 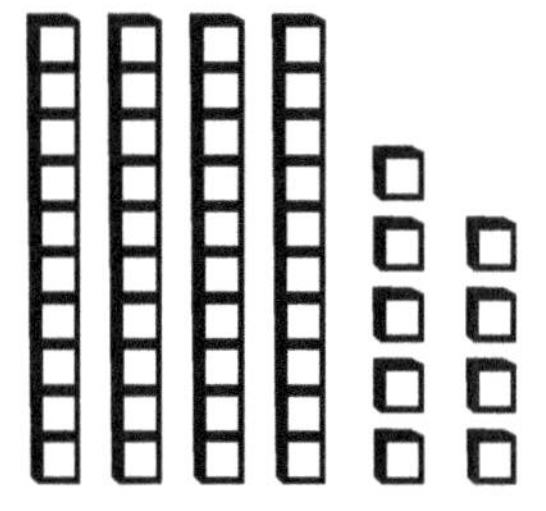

_____ tens + _____ ones

Number: _____________

18. 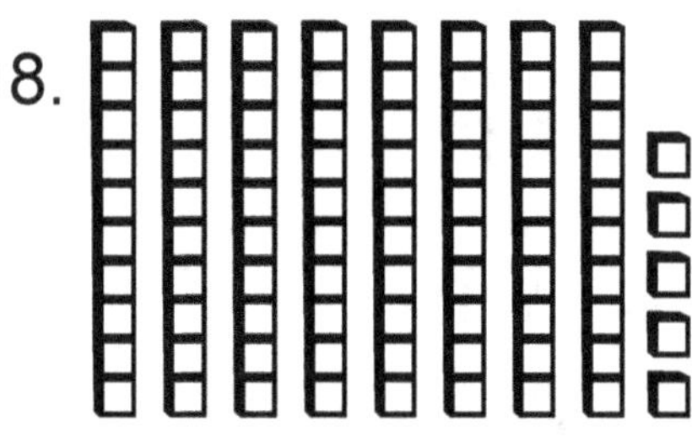

_____ tens + _____ ones

Number: _____________

# BRAIN STRETCH

Circle the larger number in each set.

32  49        8  28        72  89        59  75

# Writing Numbers in Different Ways

Circle two correct ways to make each number.

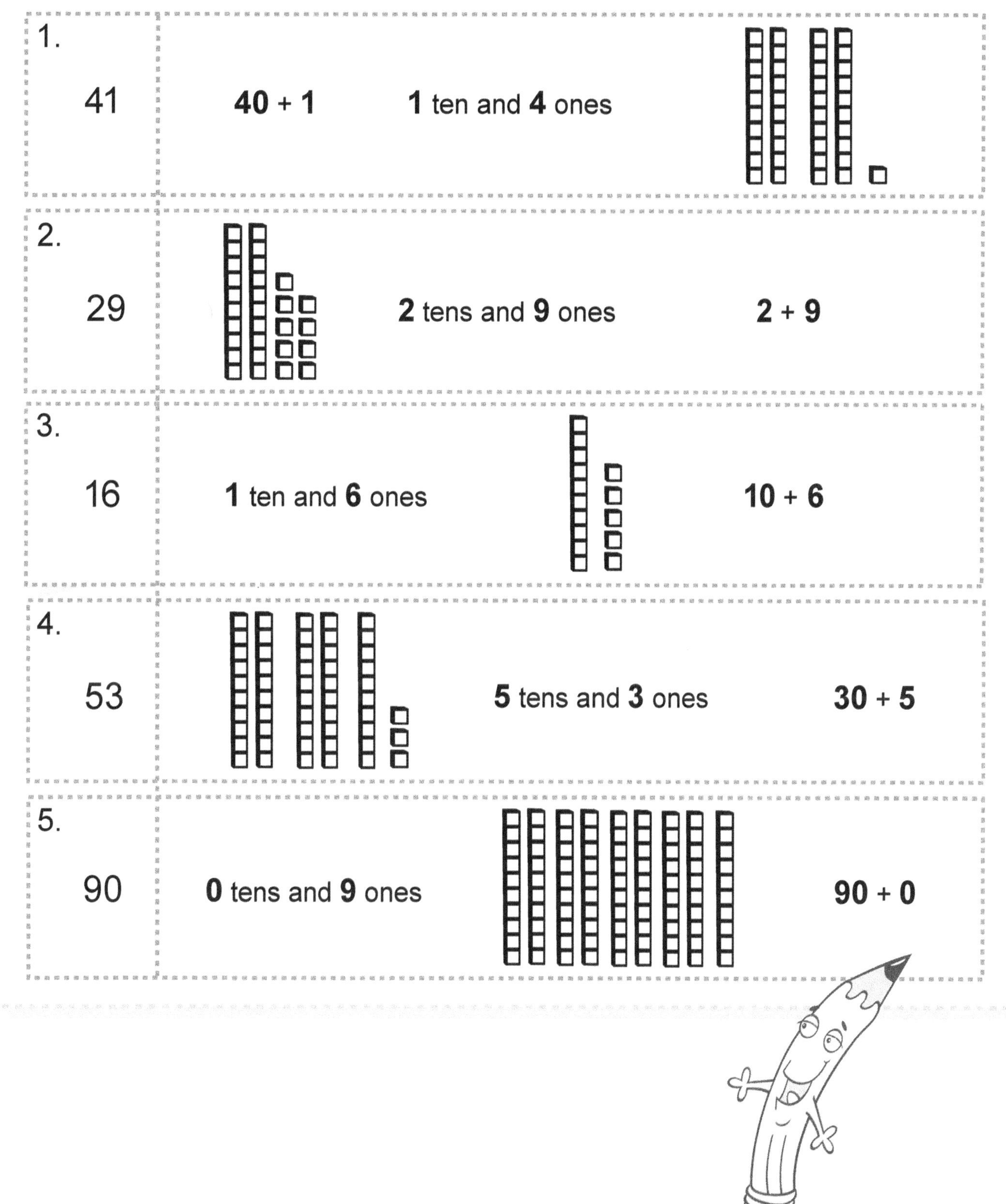

# Writing Numbers in Standard Form

There are different ways to write a number.

10 + 7

1 ten + 7 ones

seventeen

17

17 is written in standard form.

Write each number in standard form.

1.  40 + 5 _______________________________

2.  7 tens  6 ones _______________________________

3.  nineteen _______________________________

4.  60 + 2 _______________________________

5.  8 tens  4 ones _______________________________

6.  eleven _______________________________

7.  50 + 6 _______________________________

8.  eight _______________________________

9.  5 tens  3 ones _______________________________

10.  four _______________________________

11.  3 tens  9 ones _______________________________

12.  80 + 3 _______________________________

# Sum Fun

1. Use the color key to color the picture.

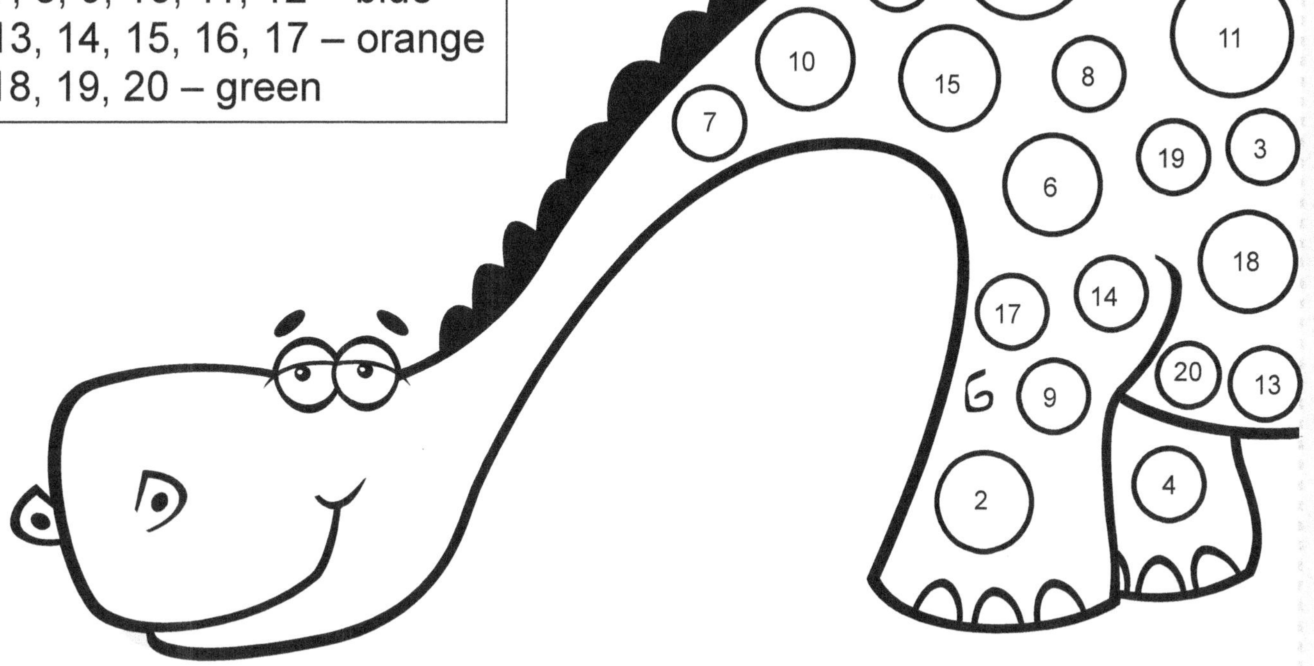



2. Complete the sums.

| | | |
|---|---|---|
| 5 + 4 = _____ | 6 + 6 = _____ | 3 + 6 = _____ |
| 1 + 7 = _____ | 0 + 1 = _____ | 9 + 5 = _____ |
| 4 + 2 = _____ | 2 + 2 = _____ | 7 + 7 = _____ |
| 7 + 3 = _____ | 4 + 1 = _____ | 2 + 1 = _____ |
| 5 + 2 = _____ | 5 + 3 = _____ | 9 + 2 = _____ |
| 10 + 10 = _____ | 8 + 2 = _____ | 9 + 9 = _____ |

# Adding 1 or 2 by Counting On

**Add 1 by counting on.**

10 + 1 = ______

Start with the greater number.

Count on by 1.

10          11

Stop when 1 finger is up.

10 + 1 = __11__

**Add 2 by counting on.**

14 + 2 = ______

Start with the greater number.

Count on by 2.

14          15          16

Stop when 2 fingers are up.

14 + 2 = __16__

1. Count on to add.

| | |
|---|---|
| 12 + 1 = ______ <br><br> 12, ______ | 7 + 2 = ______ <br><br> 7, ______, ______ |
| 23 + 1 = ______ <br><br> 23, ______ | 30 + 2 = ______ <br><br> 30, ______, ______ |
| 41 + 1 = ______ <br><br> 41, ______ | 88 + 2 = ______ <br><br> 88, ______, ______ |

# Adding 1 or 2 by Counting On (continued)

2. Count on to add.

| | |
|---|---|
| 29 + 1 = _____<br><br>29, _____ | 33 + 2 = _____<br><br>33, _____, _____ |
| 46 + 1 = _____<br><br>46, _____ | 54 + 2 = _____<br><br>54, _____, _____ |
| 19 + 1 = _____<br><br>19, _____ | 81 + 2 = _____<br><br>81, _____, _____ |
| 9 + 1 = _____<br><br>9, _____ | 25 + 2 = _____<br><br>25, _____, _____ |
| 38 + 1 = _____<br><br>38, _____ | 0 + 2 = _____<br><br>0, _____, _____ |
| 17 + 1 = _____<br><br>17, _____ | 13 + 2 = _____<br><br>13, _____, _____ |

# Addition Doubles

Write the number sentence.

1. 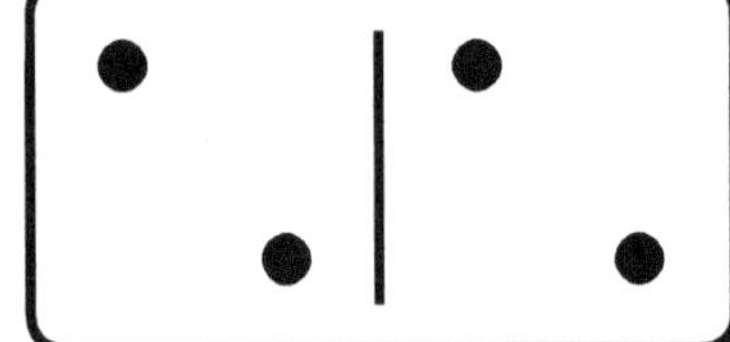  ______ + ______ = ______

2. 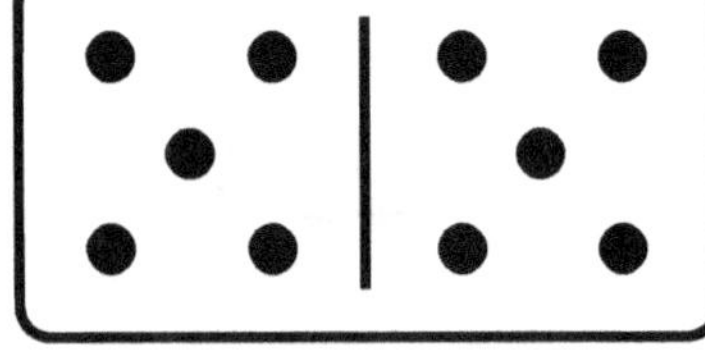  ______ + ______ = ______

3.   ______ + ______ = ______

4. 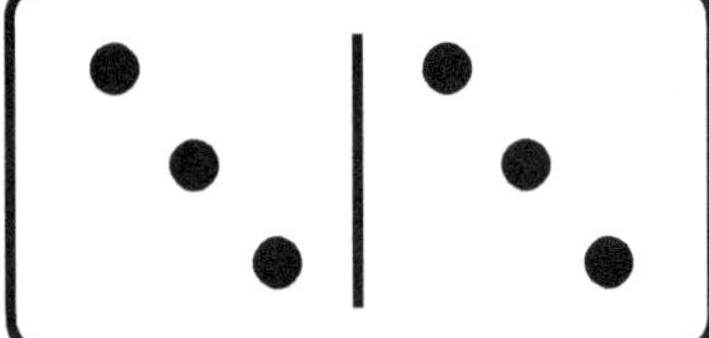  ______ + ______ = ______

5. 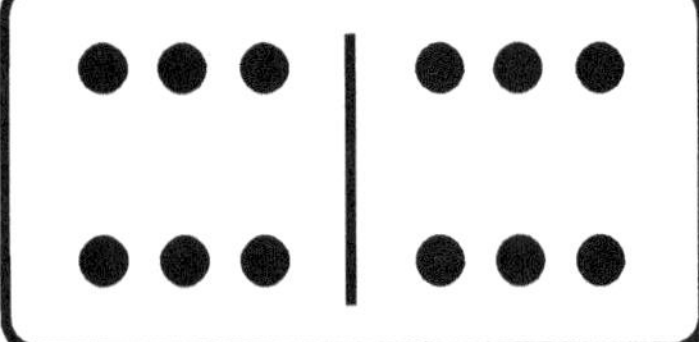  ______ + ______ = ______

6. 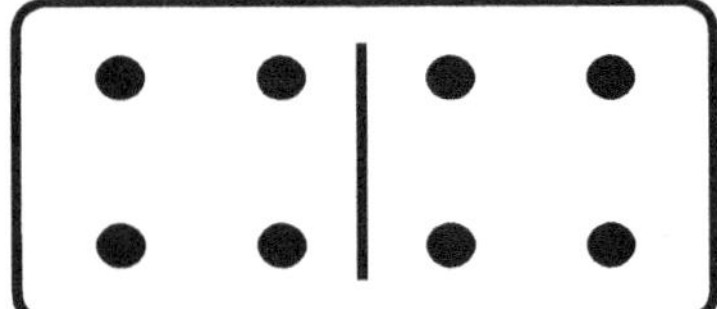  ______ + ______ = ______

# Addition Doubles Plus 1

Add using doubles plus 1.

If      6 + 6 = **12**
Then  6 + 7 = **13**

If      10 + 10 = ____
Then  ____ + ____ = ____

If      3 + 3 = ____
Then  ____ + ____ = ____

If      5 + 5 = ____
Then  ____ + ____ = ____

If      8 + 8 = ____
Then  ____ + ____ = ____

If      1 + 1 = ____
Then  ____ + ____ = ____

If      9 + 9 = ____
Then  ____ + ____ = ____

If      2 + 2 = ____
Then  ____ + ____ = ____

If      4 + 4 = ____
Then  ____ + ____ = ____

If      7 + 7 = ____
Then  ____ + ____ = ____

# Numbers Can be Added in Any Order

1. Use the ten-frames to show adding numbers in two ways. Use two different colors. Then, write the answers.

5 + 2 = **7**
2 + 5 = **7**

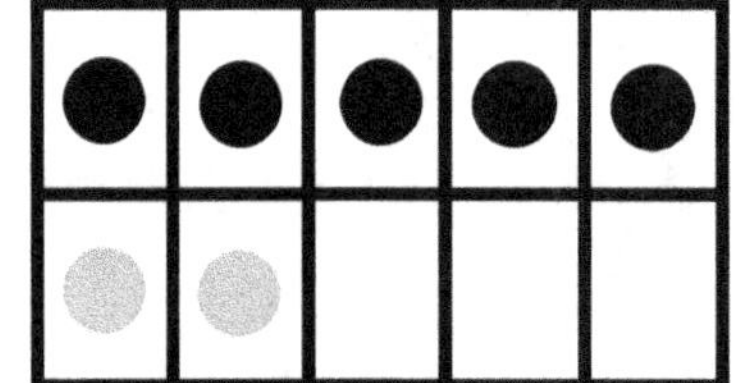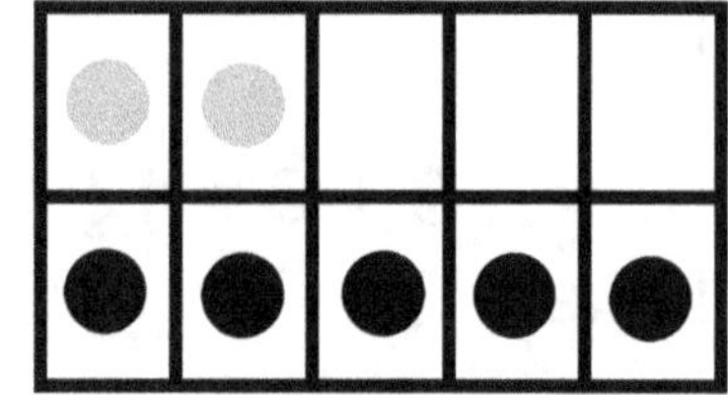

7 + 3 = ____
3 + 7 = ____

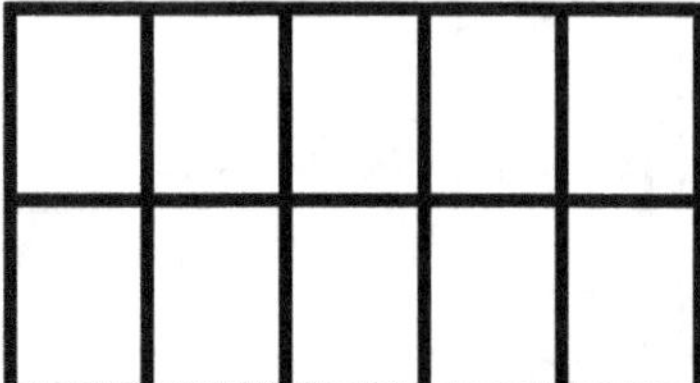

6 + 4 = ____
4 + 6 = ____

1 + 9 = ____
9 + 1 = ____

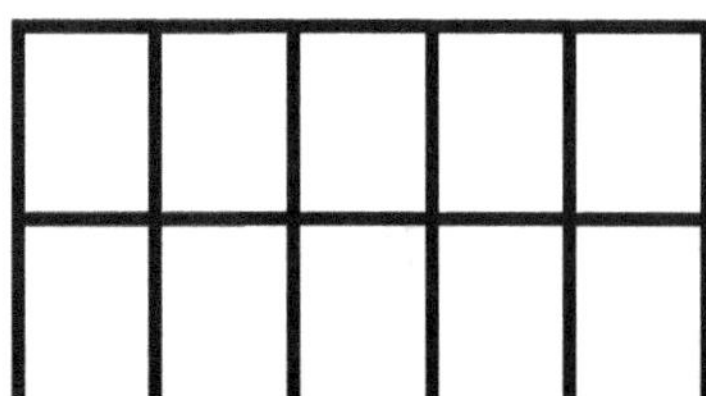

3 + 5 = ____
5 + 3 = ____

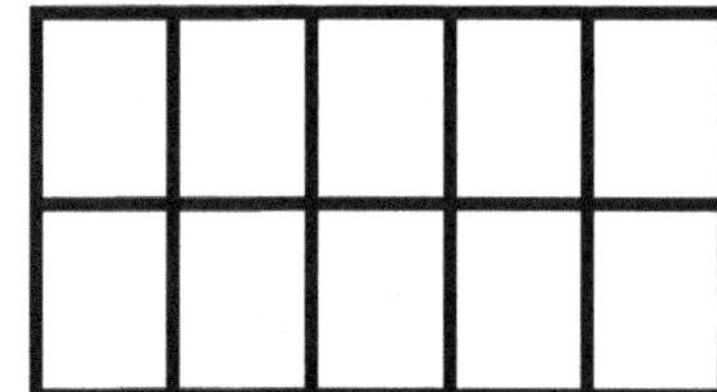

2 + 8 = ____
8 + 2 = ____

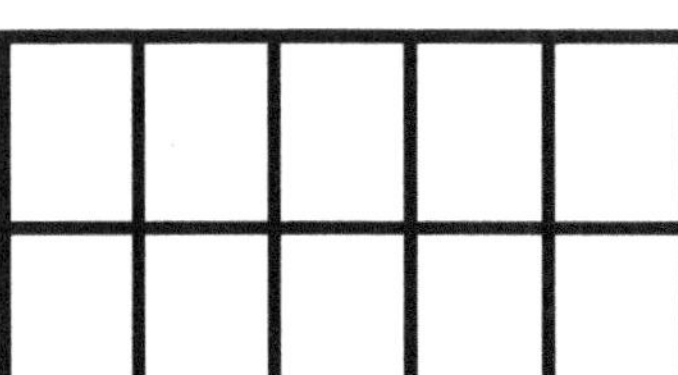

2. Use the ten-frames to show adding numbers in two ways.
   Use two different colors. Then, write the answers.

1 + 4 = _____

4 + 1 = _____

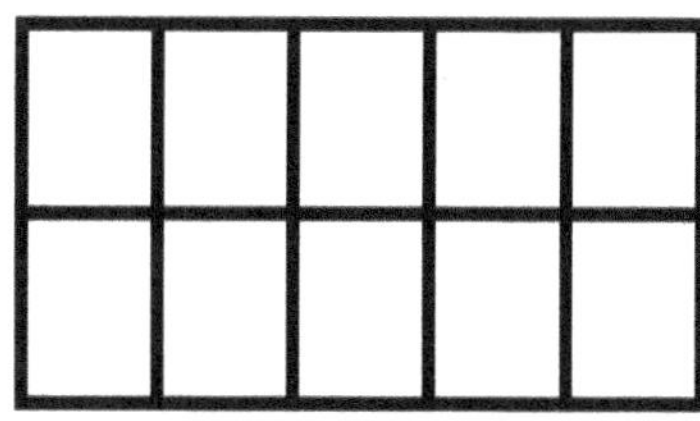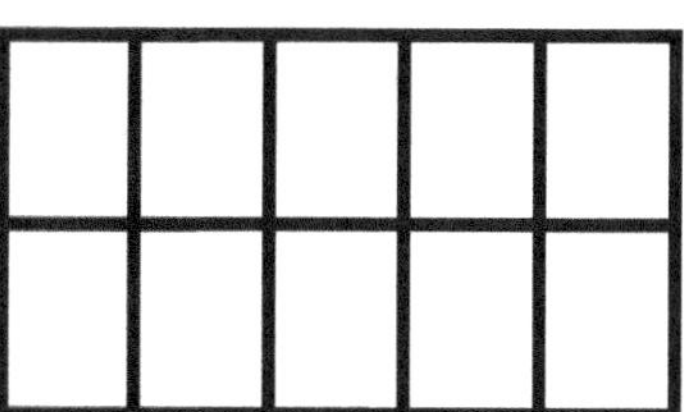

7 + 2 = _____

2 + 7 = _____

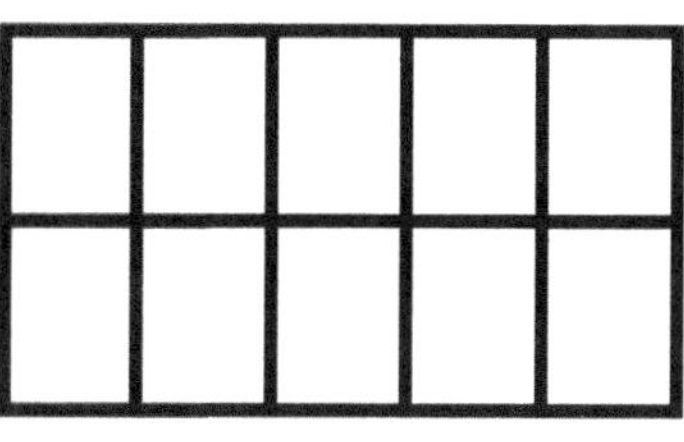

4 + 3 = _____

3 + 4 = _____

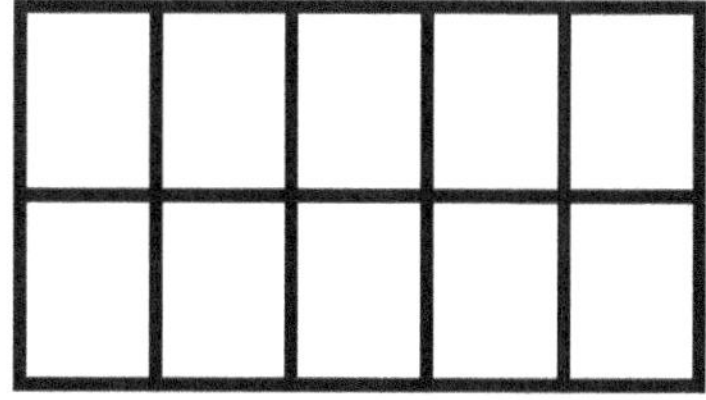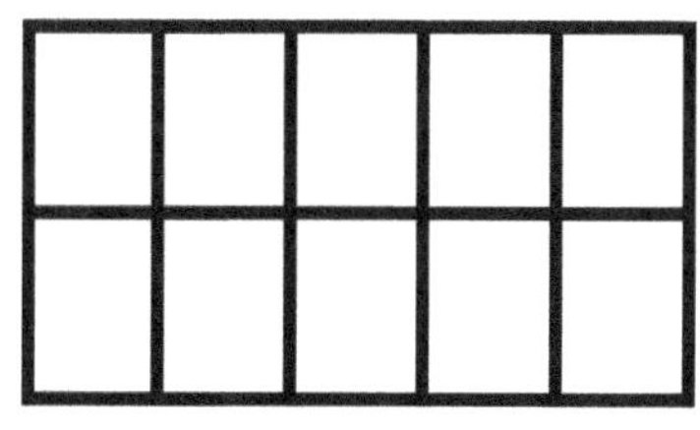

1 + 8 = _____

8 + 1 = _____

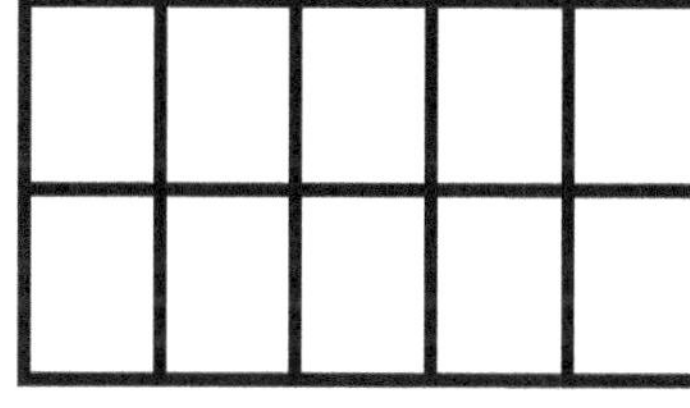

2 + 1 = _____

1 + 2 = _____

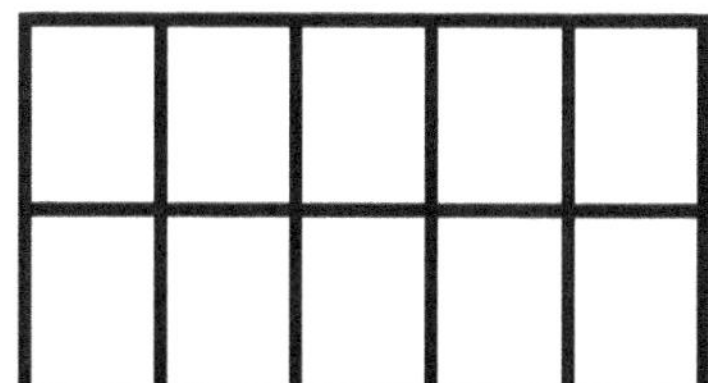

Make your own question.
Use numbers that are
less than 10.

___ + ___ = ___ + ___

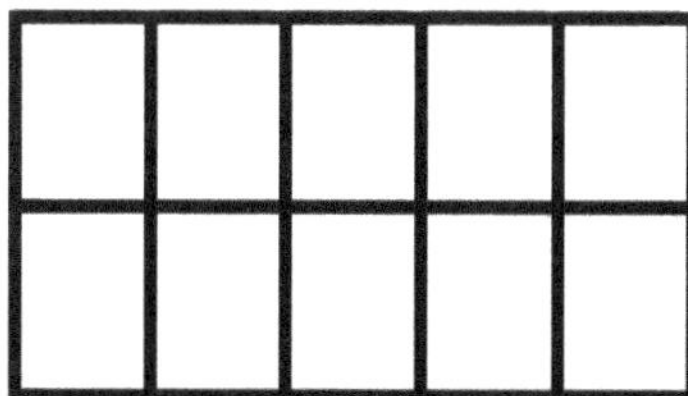

# Using a Number Line to Add

Add using a number line.

$9 + 3 =$ **12**

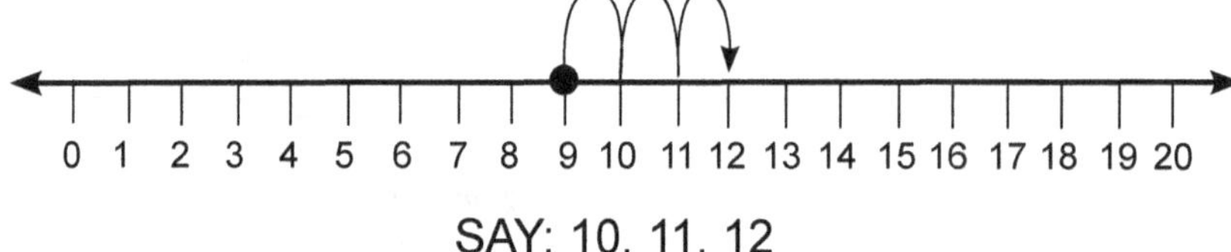



Mark a dot at 9.
Draw 3 steps to count on.
Stop at 12.

1. Use the number line to add. Mark a dot to show where to start. Next, count on by drawing the steps. Write the answer.

$9 + 7 =$ ___

$6 + 12 =$ ___

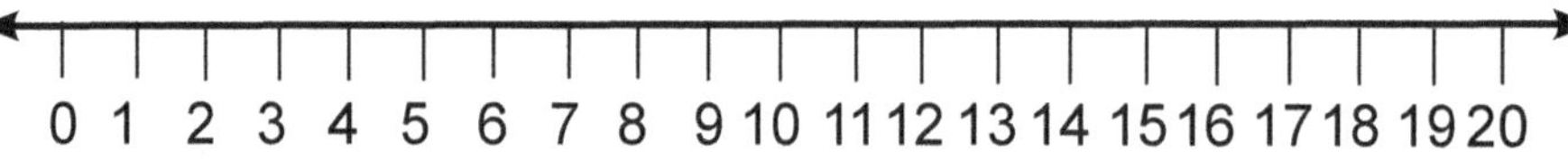



$11 + 4 =$ ___

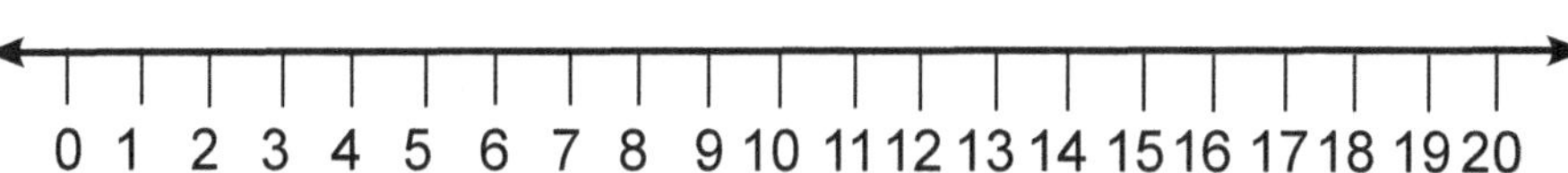



$2 + 15 =$ ___

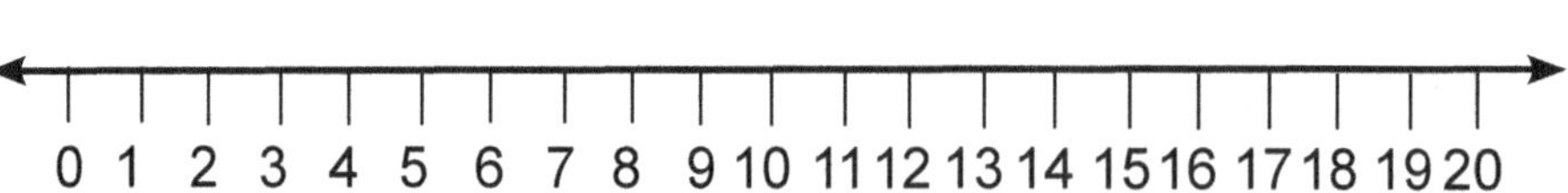

2. Use the number line to add by counting on. Mark a dot to show where to start. Next, draw the steps. Write the answer.

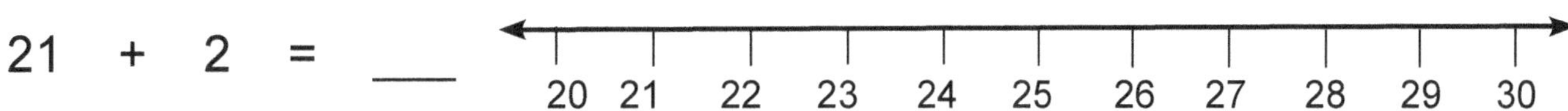

21 + 2 = ___

20  21  22  23  24  25  26  27  28  29  30

24 + 5 = ___

20  21  22  23  24  25  26  27  28  29  30

32 + 4 = ___

30  31  32  33  34  35  36  37  38  39  40

46 + 6 = ___

45  46  47  48  49  50  51  52  53  54  55

70 + 7 = ___

68  69  70  71  72  73  74  75  76  77  78

63 + 3 = ___

60  61  62  63  64  65  66  67  68  69  70

49 + 1 = ___

45  46  47  48  49  50  51  52  53  54  55

# Making 10 to Add

Use a group of 10 to help you add.

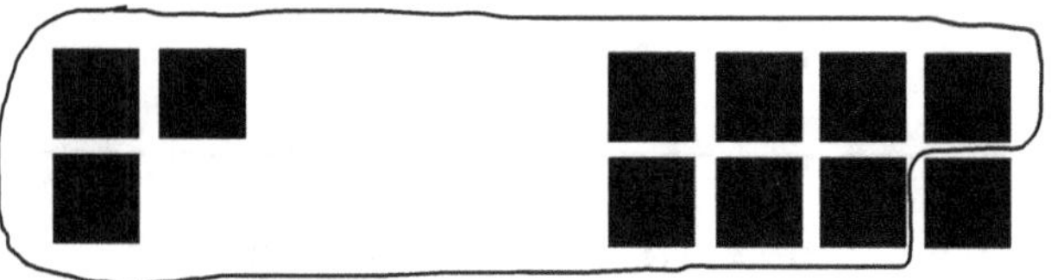

$8 + 3 = 10 + \underline{\textbf{1}} = \underline{\textbf{11}}$

Circle 10. There is 1 more block.
Use 10 to add.

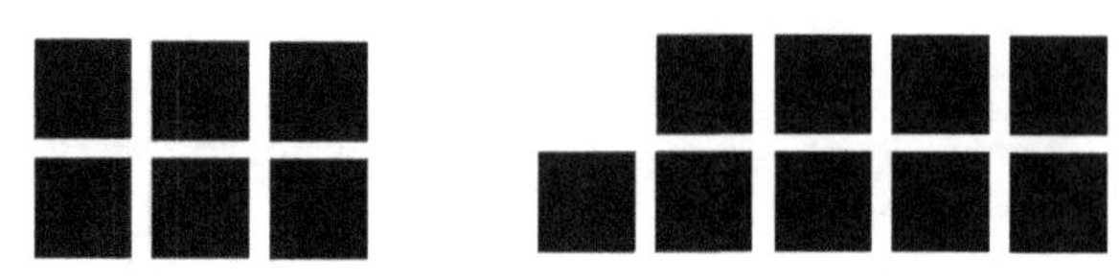

$6 + 9 = 10 + \underline{\hspace{1cm}} = \underline{\hspace{1cm}}$

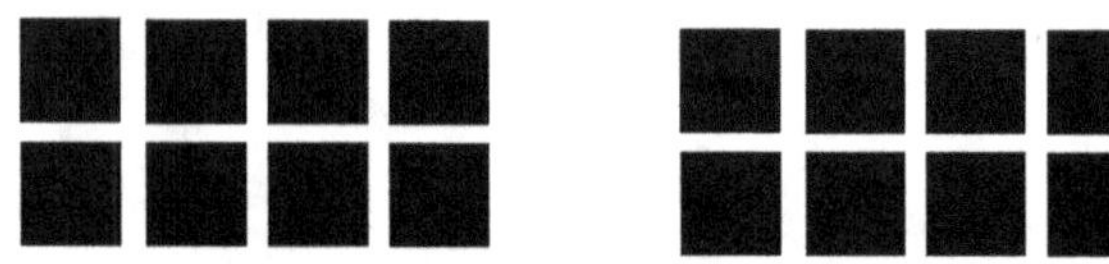

$8 + 8 = 10 + \underline{\hspace{1cm}} = \underline{\hspace{1cm}}$

$7 + 5 = 10 + \underline{\hspace{1cm}} = \underline{\hspace{1cm}}$

$14 + 4 = 10 + \underline{\hspace{1cm}} = \underline{\hspace{1cm}}$

$9 + 9 = 10 + \underline{\hspace{1cm}} = \underline{\hspace{1cm}}$

# Making Addition Sentences

1. Show three ways to make each number.
   Use two colors to color the blocks.

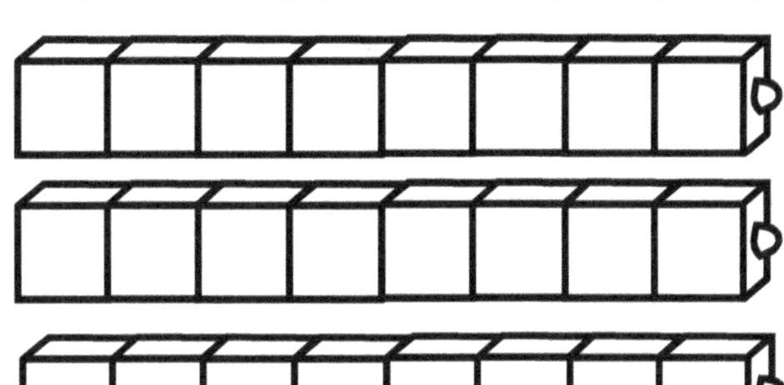

___ + ___ = 8

___ + ___ = 8

___ + ___ = 8

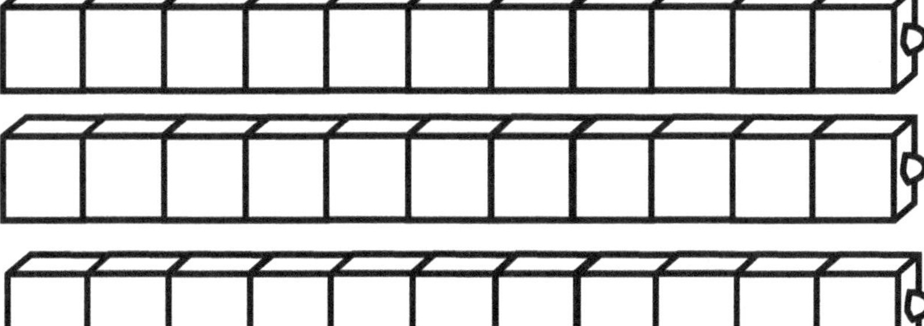

___ + ___ = 11

___ + ___ = 11

___ + ___ = 11

___ + ___ = 9

___ + ___ = 9

___ + ___ = 9

___ + ___ = 13

___ + ___ = 13

___ + ___ = 13

# Making Addition Sentences (continued)

2. Show three ways to make each number.
   Use two colors to color the blocks.

___ + ___ = 12

___ + ___ = 12

___ + ___ = 12

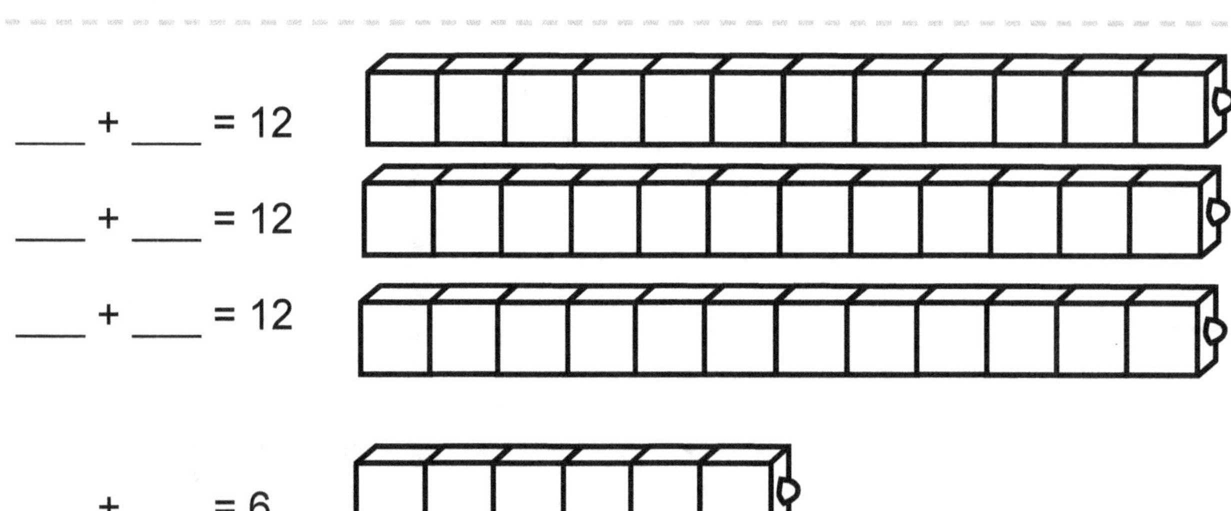

___ + ___ = 6

___ + ___ = 6

___ + ___ = 6

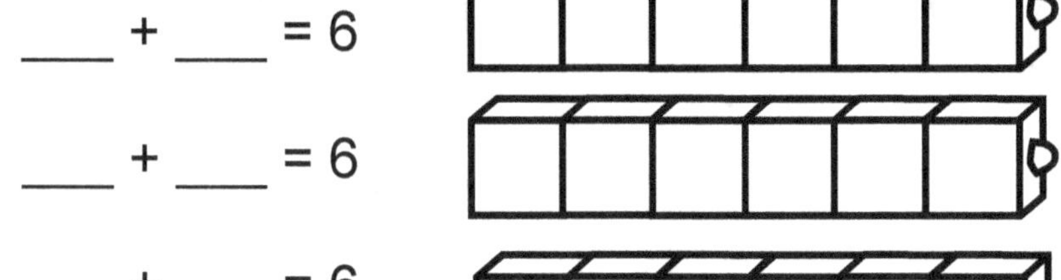
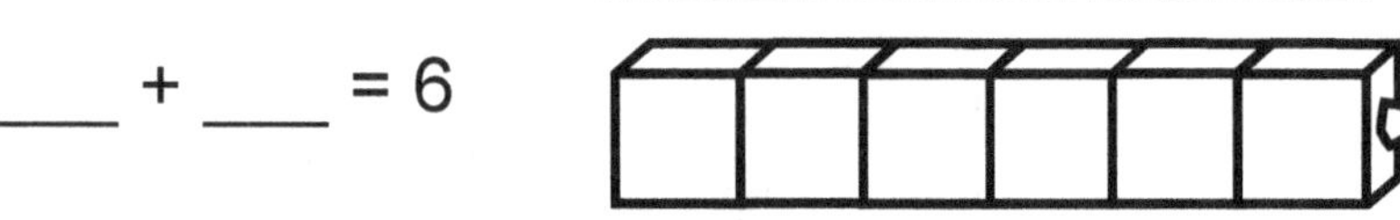

___ + ___ = 10

___ + ___ = 10

___ + ___ = 10

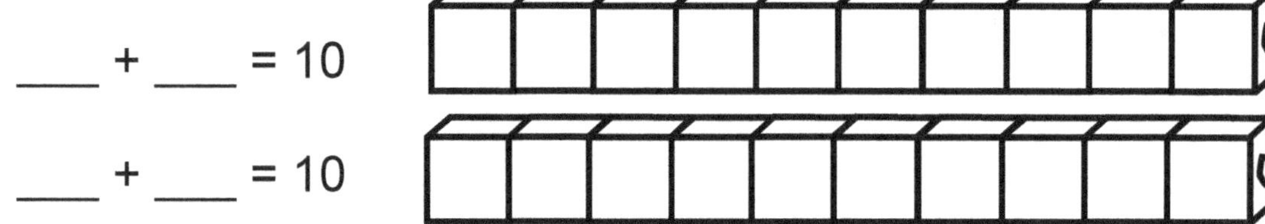

___ + ___ = 14

___ + ___ = 14

___ + ___ = 14

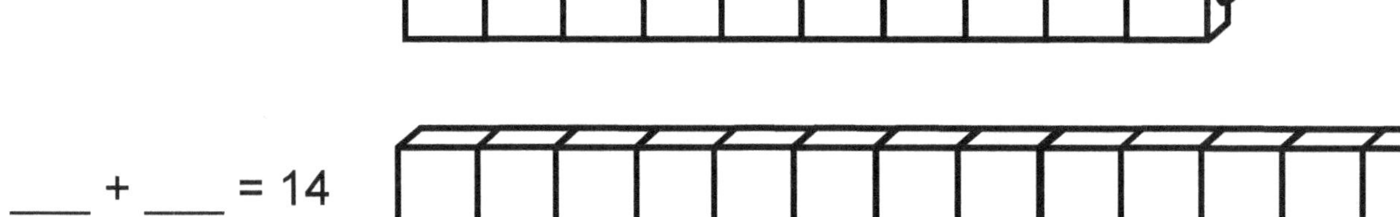

# Addition Practice

Add. Use the number line or counters to help add.

0  1  2  3  4  5  6  7  8  9  10  11  12  13  14  15  16  17  18  19  20

| 8 + 6 | 7 + 7 | 12 + 3 | 6 + 6 | 15 + 3 |
|---|---|---|---|---|
| 17 + 2 | 11 + 0 | 10 + 3 | 11 + 7 | 4 + 9 |
| 8 + 10 | 9 + 8 | 13 + 1 | 13 + 4 | 14 + 3 |
| 9 + 5 | 11 + 7 | 9 + 9 | 5 + 13 | 3 + 12 |

Fill in the missing number. Use the number line to help.

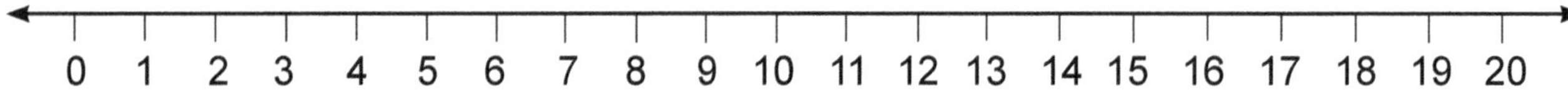


| | | | | |
|---|---|---|---|---|
| 3 + ▢ = 6 | 9 + ▢ = 18 | 3 + ▢ = 12 | ▢ + 6 = 14 | 4 + ▢ = 15 |
| 9 + ▢ = 17 | ▢ + 2 = 11 | 7 + ▢ = 12 | ▢ + 7 = 13 | 6 + ▢ = 12 |
| 3 + ▢ = 5 | 7 + ▢ = 7 | ▢ + 10 = 18 | ▢ + 9 = 14 | 1 + ▢ = 11 |
| ▢ + 8 = 16 | 10 + ▢ = 20 | ▢ + 4 = 10 | 2 + ▢ = 6 | 10 + ▢ = 15 |

# Addition Riddle

Solve the math riddle.

4 + 8 = ☐ A

10 + 10 = ☐ B

6 + 3 = ☐ C

5 + 5 = ☐ D

4 + 2 = ☐ E

2 + 2 = ☐ G

2 + 9 = ☐ H

8 + 10 = ☐ I

9 + 6 = ☐ L

8 + 5 = ☐ N

10 + 7 = ☐ R

7 + 9 = ☐ S

6 + 1 = ☐ T

2 + 6 = ☐ U

7 + 7 = ☐ W

3 + 0 = ☐ Y

___ ___ ___ ___ ___ ___ ___ | ___ ___ ___ | ___ ___ ___ ___ ___ ___ ___ ___ |
20  6  9  12  8  16  6 | 11  6  17 | 16  7  8  10  6  13  7  16 |

___ ___ ___ | ___ ___ ___ ___ ___ ___ | ___ ___ ___ ___ ___ ___ !
14  6  17  6 | 17  6  12  15  15  3 | 20  17  18  4  11  7

# Addition Word Problems

Solve the problems.

1. There were 6  in the pan.

   Pam adds 2 more  .

   How many are there altogether? _______ + _______ = _______

   There are _______ altogether.

2. There were 8  on the ground.

   Then 7 more  come.

   How many are there in total? _______ + _______ = _______

   There are _______ in total.

3. There are 12  on the branch.

   Then 2 more come.

   How many are there altogether? _______ + _______ = _______

   There are _______ altogether.

4. There are 13  in the pond.
   Then 3 more  come.

   How many are there in all? _______ + _______ = _______

   There are _______ in all.

# Subtracting 1 or 2 by Counting Back

<table>
<tr><td>

**Subtract 1 by counting back.**

5 − 1 = _____

Count back from the first number.

Count out loud.

  5       4

Stop when 1 finger is up.

5 − 1 = __4__

</td><td>

**Subtract 2 by counting back.**

7 − 2 = _____

Count back from the first number.

Count out loud.

  7    6    5

Stop when 2 fingers are up.

7 − 2 = __5__

</td></tr>
</table>

1. Subtract by counting back.

| | |
|---|---|
| 8 − 1 = ____<br><br>8, ____ | 9 − 2 = ____<br><br>9, ____, ____ |
| 17 − 1 = ____<br><br>17, ____ | 14 − 2 = ____<br><br>14, ____, ____ |
| 15 − 1 = ____<br><br>15, ____ | 16 − 2 = ____<br><br>16, ____, ____ |
| 13 − 1 = ____<br><br>13, ____ | 19 − 2 = ____<br><br>19, ____, ____ |

2. Count back to subtract.

| | |
|---|---|
| 18 − 1 = ______ <br><br> 18, ______ | 11 − 2 = ______ <br><br> 11, ______, ______ |
| 29 − 1 = ______ <br><br> 29, ______ | 20 − 2 = ______ <br><br> 20, ______, ______ |
| 12 − 1 = ______ <br><br> 12, ______ | 33 − 2 = ______ <br><br> 33, ______, ______ |
| 44 − 1 = ______ <br><br> 44, ______ | 25 − 2 = ______ <br><br> 25, ______, ______ |
| 66 − 1 = ______ <br><br> 66, ______ | 58 − 2 = ______ <br><br> 58, ______, ______ |
| 52 − 1 = ______ <br><br> 52, ______ | 42 − 2 = ______ <br><br> 42, ______, ______ |
| 61 − 1 = ______ <br><br> 61, ______ | 87 − 2 = ______ <br><br> 87, ______, ______ |

# Subtraction Fun

1. Use the key to color the picture.

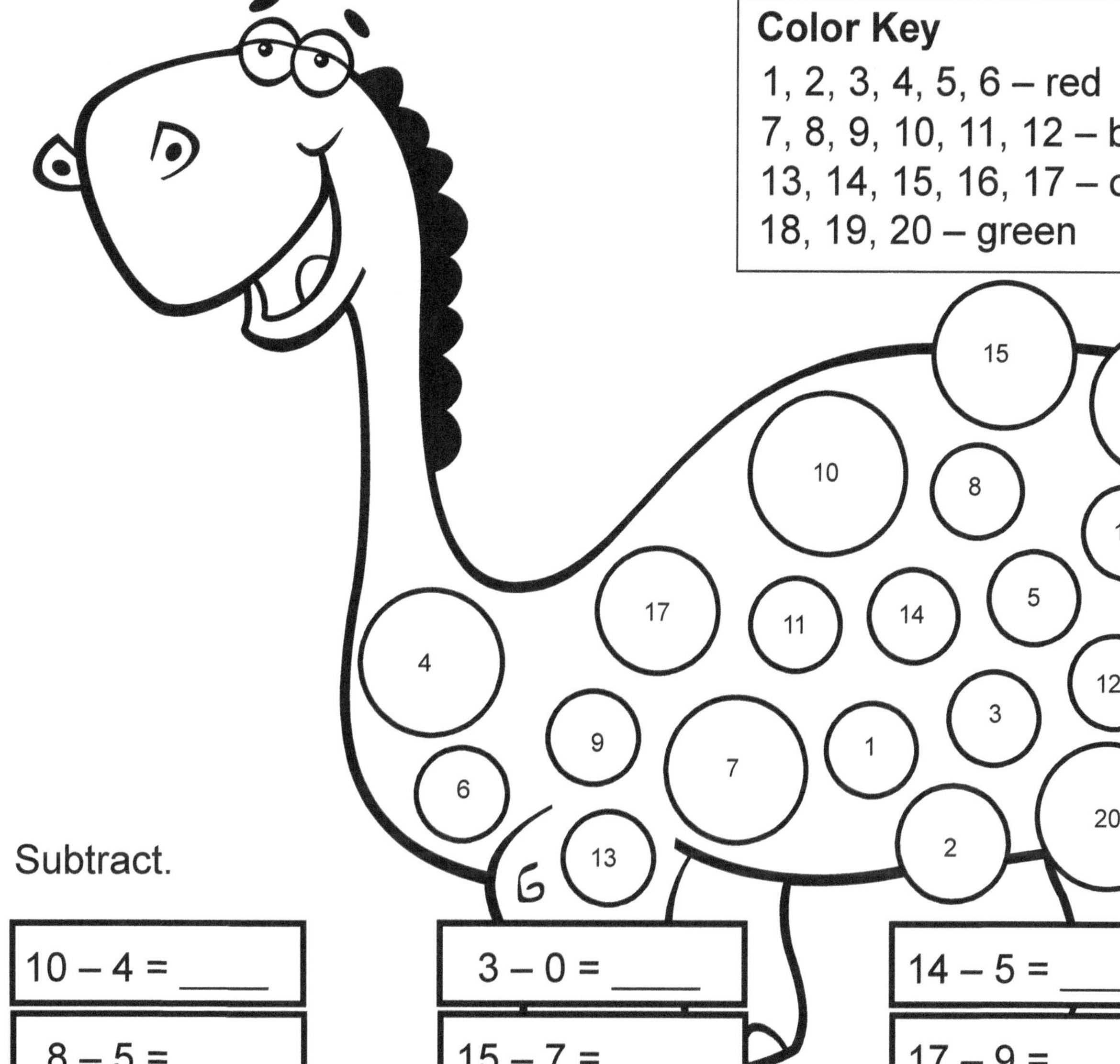



2. Subtract.

| | | |
|---|---|---|
| 10 – 4 = _____ | 3 – 0 = _____ | 14 – 5 = _____ |
| 8 – 5 = _____ | 15 – 7 = _____ | 17 – 9 = _____ |
| 6 – 3 = _____ | 9 – 2 = _____ | 12 – 6 = _____ |
| 2 – 1 = _____ | 16 – 8 = _____ | 7 – 1 = _____ |
| 13 – 7 = _____ | 5 – 4 = _____ | 18 – 9 = _____ |
| 10 – 10 = _____ | 11 – 3 = _____ | 4 – 1 = _____ |

# Using a Number Line to Subtract

Subtract using a number line.

12 – 3 = __9__

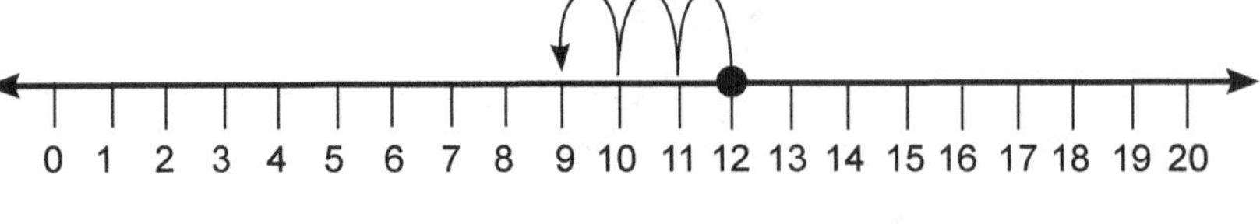

SAY: 11, 10, 9

Mark a dot at 12.
Draw 3 steps to count back.
Stop at 9.

1. Use the number line to subtract. Mark a dot to show where you start. Next, count back by drawing the steps. Write the answer.

19 – 6 = _____

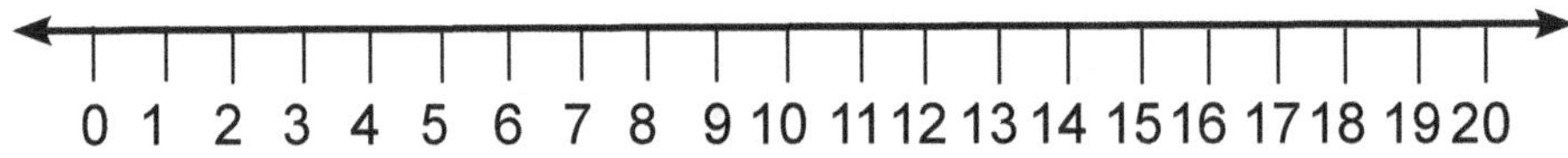

16 – 3 = _____

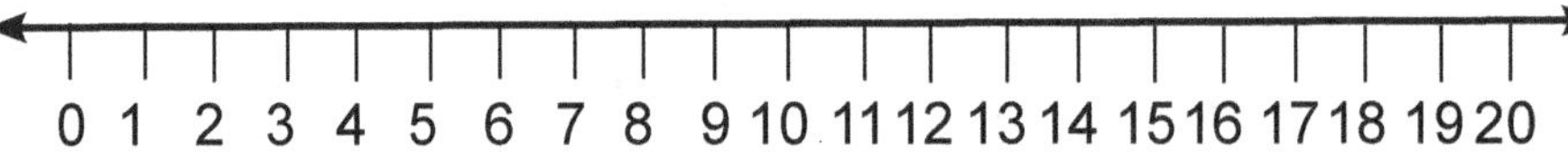

14 – 4 = _____

17 – 1 = _____

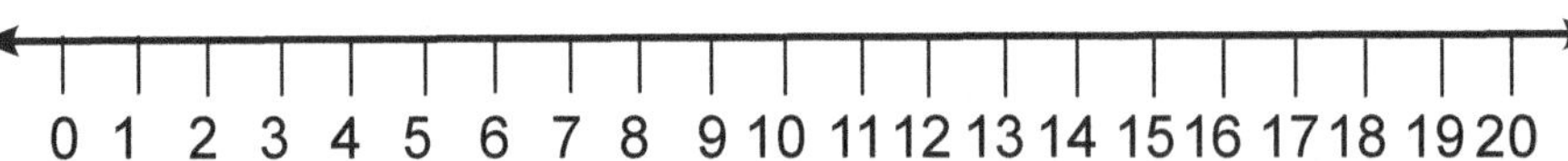

2. Use the number line to subtract. Mark a dot to show where you start. Next, count back by drawing the steps. Write the answer.

24 – 2 = _____

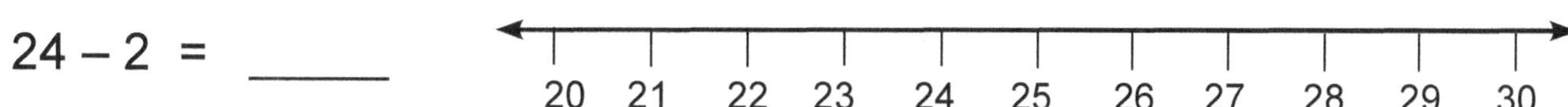

33 – 3 = _____

46 – 3 = _____

55 – 4 = _____

22 – 5 = _____

31 – 7 = _____

62 – 8 = _____

# Making Subtraction Sentences

1. Cross out the blocks you want to take away. Color the blocks left.
   Complete the subtraction sentence.

4 – ___ = ___

4 – ___ = ___

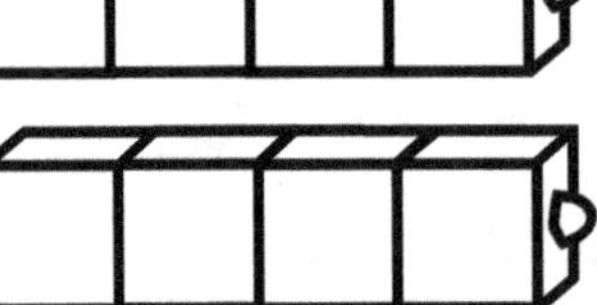

4 – ___ = ___

6 – ___ = ___

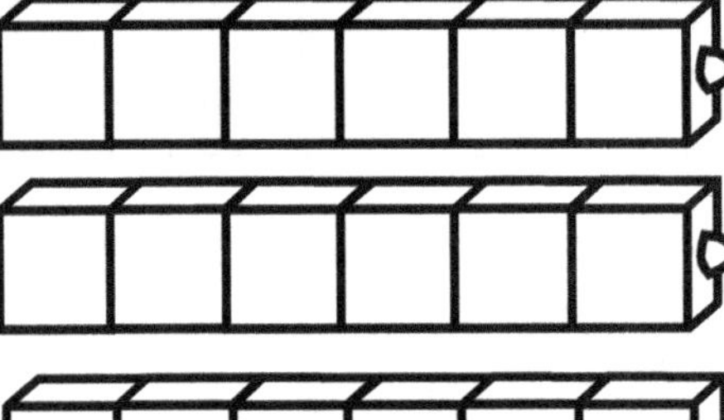

6 – ___ = ___

6 – ___ = ___

9 – ___ = ___

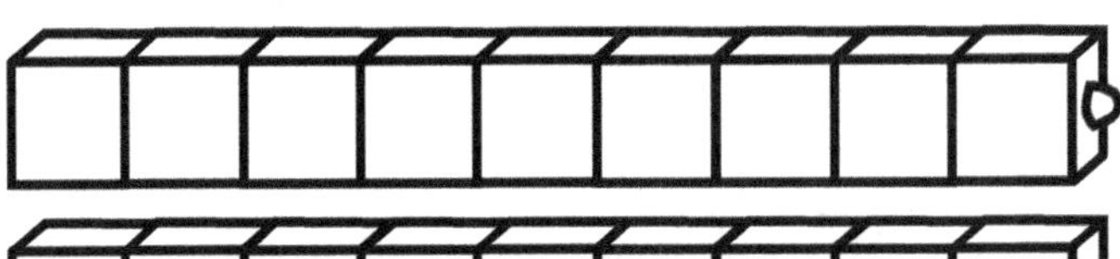

9 – ___ = ___

9 – ___ = ___

10 – ___ = ___

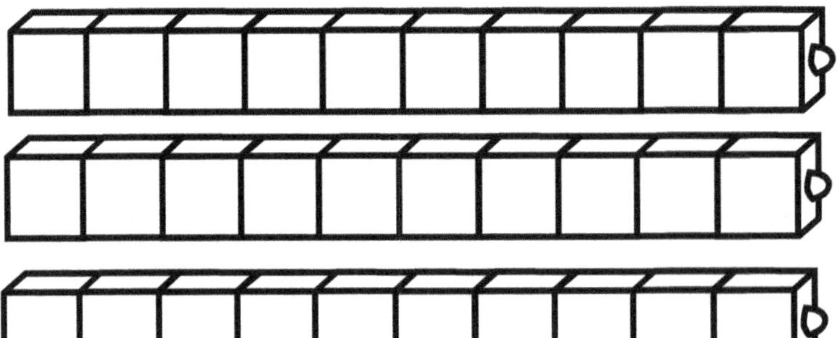

10 – ___ = ___

10 – ___ = ___



© Chalkboard Publishing

# Making Subtraction Sentences (continued)

2. Cross out the blocks you want to take away. Color the blocks left. Complete the subtraction sentence.

8 – ___ = ___

8 – ___ = ___

8 – ___ = ___

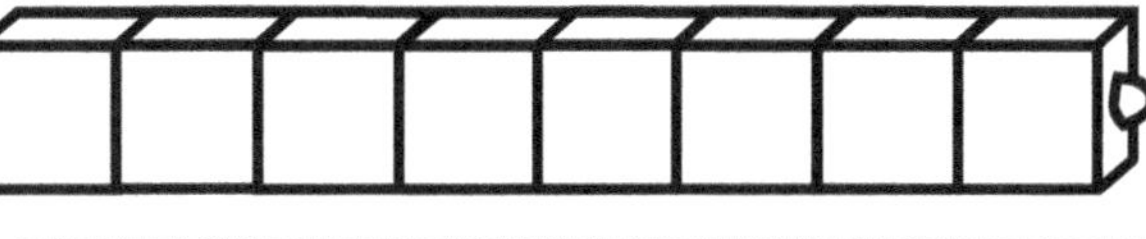

5 – ___ = ___

5 – ___ = ___

5 – ___ = ___

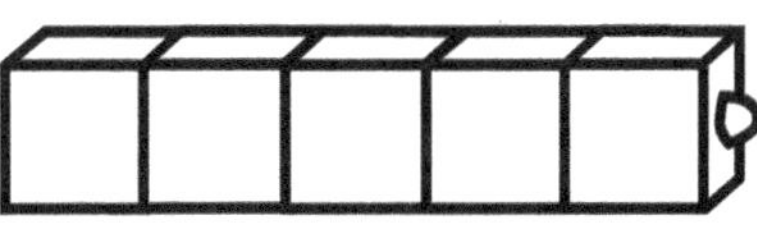
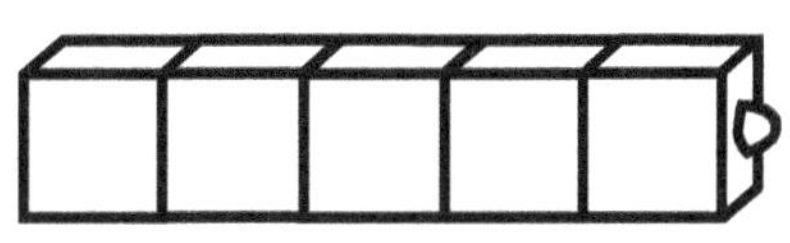

12 – ___ = ___

12 – ___ = ___

12 – ___ = ___

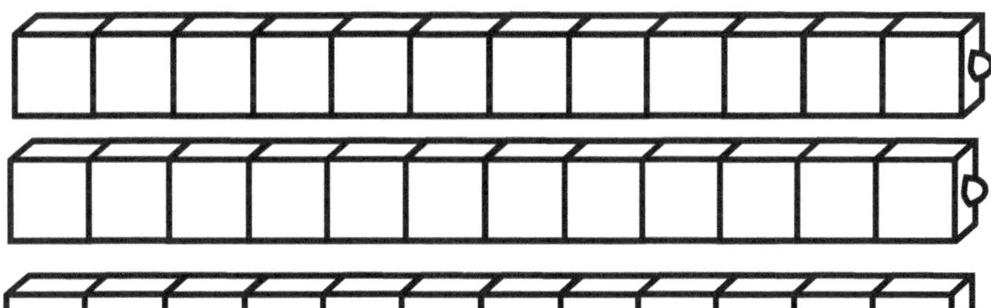

7 – ___ = ___

7 – ___ = ___

7 – ___ = ___

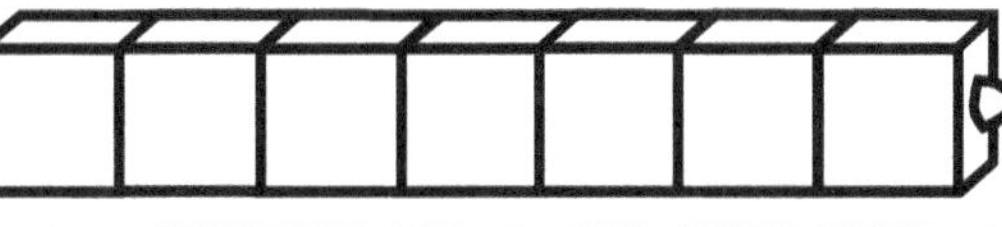
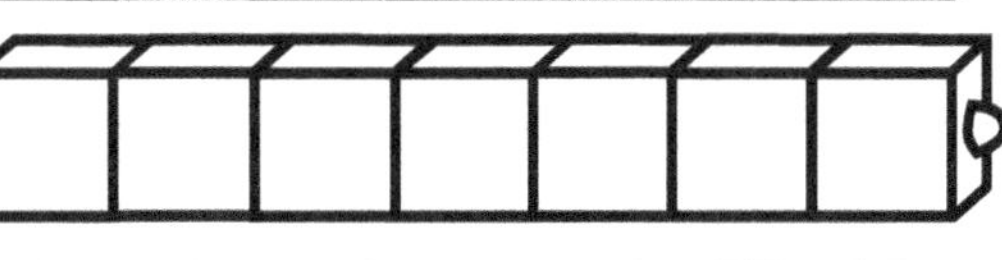

# Subtraction Practice

1. Subtract. Use the number line to help.

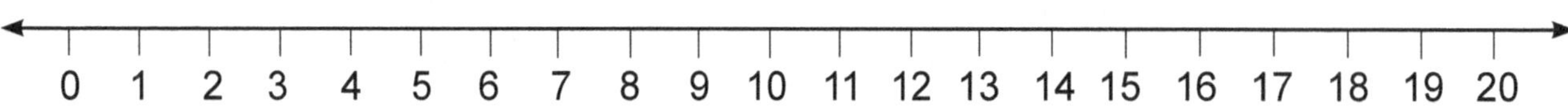



|  7  |  6  |  5  |  4  |  8  |
|:---:|:---:|:---:|:---:|:---:|
| − 3 | − 2 | − 5 | − 0 | − 3 |

|  14  |  11  |  14  |  16  |  10  |
|:----:|:----:|:----:|:----:|:----:|
| − 1  | − 3  | − 8  | − 9  | − 2  |

|  15  |  7  |  18  |  13  |  5  |
|:----:|:---:|:----:|:----:|:---:|
| − 6  | − 0 | − 8  | − 6  | − 4 |

|  12  |  8  |  16  |  9  |  11  |
|:----:|:---:|:----:|:---:|:-----:|
| − 6  | − 2 | − 8  | − 2 | − 9  |

2. Find each difference.

| 13 | 12 | 2 | 8 | 11 |
|---|---|---|---|---|
| − 7 | − 8 | − 1 | − 0 | − 4 |

| 17 | 9 | 16 | 18 | 10 |
|---|---|---|---|---|
| − 10 | − 3 | − 2 | − 9 | − 10 |

| 9 | 11 | 6 | 15 | 10 |
|---|---|---|---|---|
| − 4 | − 8 | − 3 | − 7 | − 9 |

| 4 | 11 | 3 | 16 | 7 |
|---|---|---|---|---|
| − 3 | − 2 | − 2 | − 10 | − 7 |

## BRAIN STRETCH 

12 − 4 − 3 = _____          18 − 9 − 5 = _____

14 − 8 − 2 = _____          17 − 2 − 6 = _____

# Missing Numbers

Fill in the missing numbers to complete the differences.
Use the number line to help.

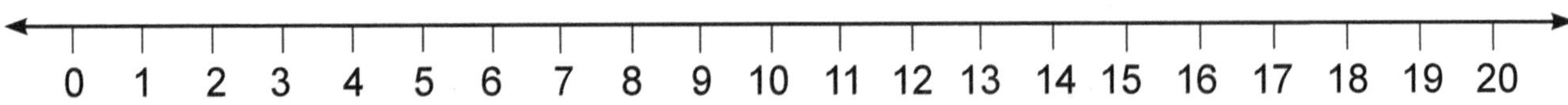



Row 1:

- ☐ − 2 = 5
- 1 − ☐ = 1
- 5 − ☐ = 2
- ☐ − 7 = 8
- 9 − ☐ = 6

Row 2:

- 13 − ☐ = 4
- 17 − ☐ = 9
- ☐ − 10 = 10
- ☐ − 9 = 6
- 8 − ☐ = 5

Row 3:

- ☐ − 10 = 7
- 3 − ☐ = 2
- ☐ − 4 = 10
- 12 − ☐ = 6
- 10 − ☐ = 5

# Subtraction Riddle

Solve the math riddle.

7 – 6 = ☐ W

13 – 7 = ☐ A

7 – 4 = ☐ B

10 – 8 = ☐ I

6 – 1 = ☐ N

8 – 4 = ☐ O

16 – 8 = ☐ R

$$\underline{\phantom{x}}\ \underline{\phantom{x}}\ \underline{\phantom{x}}\ \underline{\phantom{x}}\ \underline{\phantom{x}}\ \underline{\phantom{x}}\ \underline{\phantom{x}}\ \underline{\phantom{x}}\ !$$

6 | 8  6  2  5  3  4  1

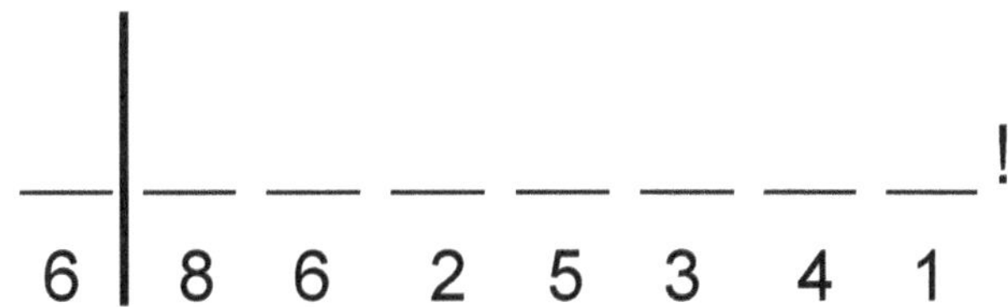

# BRAIN STRETCH

Draw a line from the number word to its matching number.

| | |
|---|---|
| sixteen | 19 |
| twelve | 16 |
| nineteen | 12 |

# Subtraction Word Problems

Solve the problems.

1. There were 7  in the pan.

   Pam ate 2 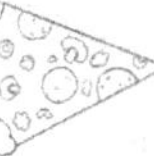.

   How many are left? _____ – _____ = _____

   There are _____ left.

2. There were 10  on the ground.

   Then 3  went away.

   How many are left? _____ – _____ = _____

   There are _____ left.

3. There were 12  on the branch.

   Then 3  flew away.

   How many are left? _____ – _____ = _____

   There are _____ left.

4. There were 15  in the pond.
   Then 5  hopped out.

   How many are left? _____ – _____ = _____

   There are _____ left.

# Word Problems

Write an addition or subtraction sentence to solve each word problem.

1. Dave had 11 boxes of crayons. He gave 5 of them to his friends. How many boxes of crayons are left?

   _____ ☐ _____ = _____

2. Abby had 12 cookies. She gave 8 cookies to her sister. How many cookies are left?

   _____ ☐ _____ = _____

3. Val bought 6 daisies and 9 tulips. How many flowers did she buy in all?

   _____ ☐ _____ = _____

4. Nicole had 18 jelly beans. She gave 8 jelly beans to Sam. How many jelly beans does Nicole have left?

   _____ ☐ _____ = _____

5. Bob had 12 pieces of bubble gum. He gave 5 pieces of bubble gum to Sally. How many pieces are left?

   _____ ☐ _____ = _____

6. Marci has 3 cats and 7 hamsters. How many pets does she have altogether?

   _____ ☐ _____ = _____

7. Jim has 14 baseball cards. He gave 4 to Nicole. How many are left?

   _____ ☐ _____ = _____

# Adding or Subtracting

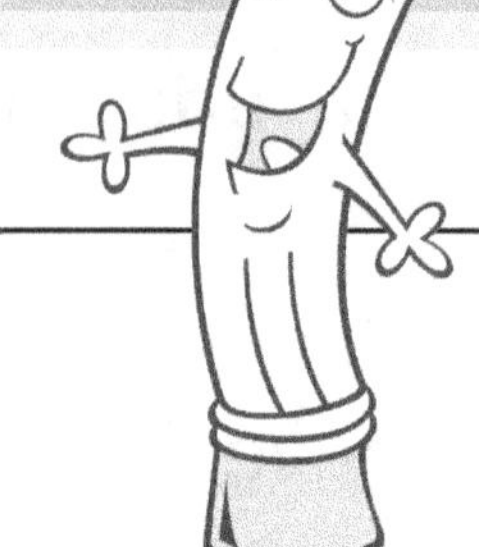

Use the number line to help find the sum or difference.

You can find the sum of two numbers by counting on.
14 + 5 = 19     Count: 14, 15, 16, 17, 18, 19

You can find the difference between two numbers by counting back.
29 − 4 = 25     Count: 29, 28, 27, 26, 25

26 + 3 =          17 + 2 =          16 − 5 =

27 − 5 =          18 + 9 =          18 + 2 =

16 − 3 =          29 − 8 =          22 + 6 =

16 + 5 =          30 − 5 =          19 − 1 =

18 + 7 =          15 + 7 =          11 − 4 =

28 − 9 =          2 + 25 =          13 − 7 =

# Ordinal Numbers to 10

An ordinal number tells the position of something in a list.

1. Write the ordinals. Hint: Use the **bold** part to help you.

fir**st** __1st__   seco**nd** __________   thi**rd** __________

fou**rth** __________   fif**th** __________   six**th** __________

seven**th** __________   eigh**th** __________   nin**th** __________

2. Circle the first 4 blocks. Cross out the last block. Color the sixth block.

3. Answer the questions.

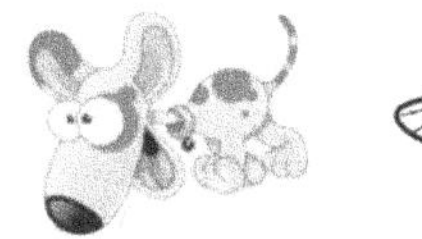     

Who is 2nd in line? __________

Who is between the 3rd and 5th animal? __________

Who is 6th in line? __________

# BRAIN STRETCH

Mark the second bird with an X. Circle the fourth bird.

# Adding Tens and Ones

Add using tens and ones.

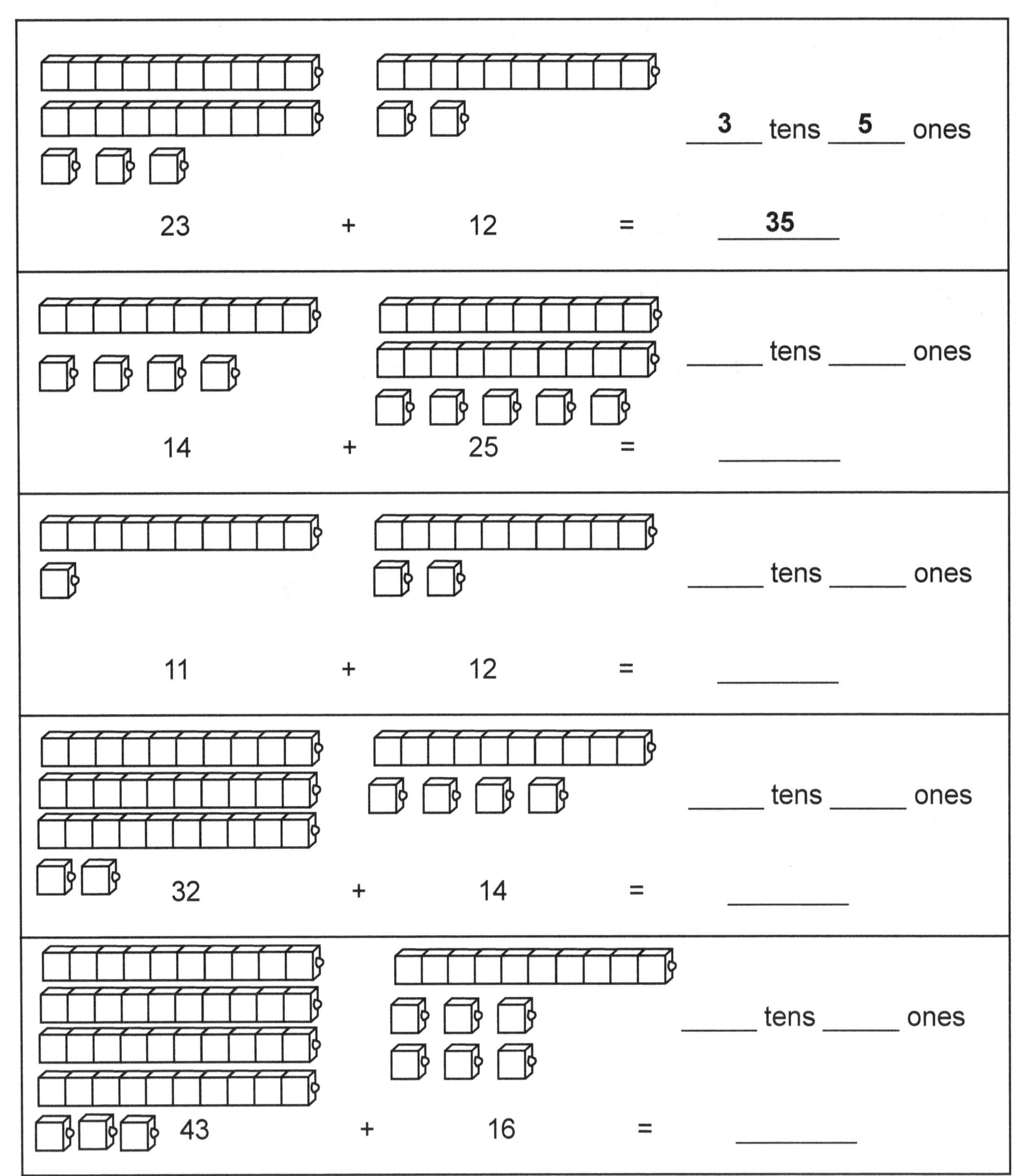

# Taking Apart to Make 10

9 + 5 = ___ 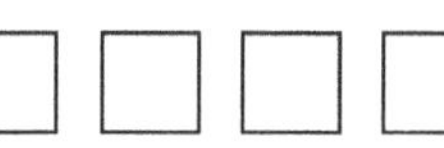

9 + 5 = 10 + 4 = 14

I know 9 + 1 = 10, so I broke 5 into 1 and 4.
Then I have to add 4 more. The sum is 14.

---

1. Use 10 to add.

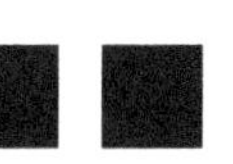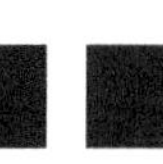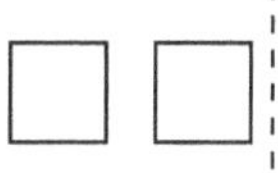

8 + 6 = 10 + ___ = ___

2. Draw a model. Use 10 to add.

7 + 8 = 10 + ___ = ___

6 + 9 = 10 + ___ = ___

9 + 7 = 10 + ___ = ___

3. Draw a model. Use 10 to add.

$4 + 9 = 10 + \underline{\phantom{00}} = \underline{\phantom{00}}$

$8 + 7 = 10 + \underline{\phantom{00}} = \underline{\phantom{00}}$

$3 + 9 = 10 + \underline{\phantom{00}} = \underline{\phantom{00}}$

$8 + 8 = 10 + \underline{\phantom{00}} = \underline{\phantom{00}}$

$5 + 7 = 10 + \underline{\phantom{00}} = \underline{\phantom{00}}$

# Two-Digit Addition Without Regrouping



| Line up the ones and tens. | First add the ones. | Then add the tens. |
|---|---|---|

First add the ones.

| tens | ones |
|---|---|
| 2 | 3 |
| + 4 | 5 |
|  | 8 |

Then add the tens.

| tens | ones |
|---|---|
| 2 | 3 |
| + 4 | 5 |
| 6 | 8 |

1. Use a tens and ones chart to help add. Shade the ones column yellow. Shade the tens column orange.

| 5 | 4 | | 2 | 2 | | 7 | 1 | | 3 | 5 | | 4 | 4 |
|---|---|---|---|---|---|---|---|---|---|---|---|---|---|
| + 3 | 1 | | + 1 | 5 | | + 2 | 7 | | + 6 | 2 | | + 3 | 0 |

| 1 | 2 | | 7 | 6 | | 6 | 2 | | 8 | 4 | | 3 | 3 |
|---|---|---|---|---|---|---|---|---|---|---|---|---|---|
| + 5 | 0 | | + 1 | 2 | | + 2 | 3 | | + 1 | 1 | | + 1 | 3 |

| 5 | 4 | | 3 | 1 | | 5 | 3 | | 6 | 2 | | 1 | 4 |
|---|---|---|---|---|---|---|---|---|---|---|---|---|---|
| + 3 | 3 | | + 2 | 6 | | + 1 | 1 | | + 3 | 7 | | + 3 | 0 |

| 8 | 2 | | 1 | 2 | | 3 | 4 | | 2 | 0 | | 5 | 2 |
|---|---|---|---|---|---|---|---|---|---|---|---|---|---|
| + 1 | 5 | | + 4 | 0 | | + 1 | 4 | | + 1 | 3 | | + 4 | 3 |

**2. Use a tens and ones chart to add.**

|  |  |  |  |  |
|---|---|---|---|---|
| 8 3<br>+ 1 4 | 1 3<br>+ 4 3 | 3 5<br>+ 1 3 | 2 1<br>+ 3 2 | 5 3<br>+ 4 6 |
| 5 5<br>+ 3 0 | 2 3<br>+ 2 5 | 7 2<br>+ 2 6 | 1 6<br>+ 6 0 | 4 5<br>+ 3 2 |
| 1 3<br>+ 5 0 | 7 7<br>+ 1 1 | 6 3<br>+ 1 3 | 8 5<br>+ 1 4 | 3 4<br>+ 1 5 |
| 5 5<br>+ 2 3 | 3 2<br>+ 2 2 | 5 4<br>+ 1 2 | 4 3<br>+ 3 6 | 1 5<br>+ 3 3 |
| 7 2<br>+ 2 5 | 2 4<br>+ 3 2 | 4 5<br>+ 1 3 | 1 1<br>+ 5 5 | 8 2<br>+ 1 6 |

# Addition Riddle

Solve the math riddle.



| | | | |
|---|---|---|---|
| 62 **I**<br>+ 35 | 32 **R**<br>+ 10 | 18 **W**<br>+ 60 | 81 **L**<br>+ 11 |
| 12 **H**<br>+ 13 | 71 **T**<br>+ 14 | 52 **V**<br>+ 21 | 31 **U**<br>+ 34 |
| 21 **G**<br>+ 11 | 31 **X**<br>+ 40 | 43 **E**<br>+ 41 | 43 **O**<br>+ 31 |
| 44 **A**<br>+ 22 | 45 **B**<br>+ 51 | 32 **S**<br>+ 27 | 21 **N**<br>+ 32 |

Watch out! Some letters are not used in the riddle.

___ ___|___ ___ ___|___ ___ ___ ___ ___ ___ ___ ___|___|___ ___ ___|
25  84  78  66  59  92  84  66  42  53  97  53  32  66  53  84  78

___ ___ ___ ___ ___ ___ ___ ___  !
92  66  53  32  65  66  32  84

# Two-Digit Addition with Regrouping

Line up the ones and the tens.
Add the ones.
If there are more than 9 ones, trade 10 ones for 1 ten.
Regroup in the tens column.
Write the ones. Then write the tens.

|      | tens | ones |
|------|------|------|
|      | ¹2   | 6    |
| +    | 2    | 6    |
|      | 5    | 2    |

Trade 10 ones from 12 for 1 ten.
Regroup by writing 1 in the tens column.

1. Use a tens and ones chart to help add. Shade the ones column yellow.
   Shade the tens column orange.

| 6 4 | 2 2 | 6 5 | 3 9 | 4 4 |
|-----|-----|-----|-----|-----|
| + 1 8 | + 1 9 | + 2 7 | + 2 2 | + 3 8 |

| 1 2 | 7 6 | 6 4 | 2 9 | 3 6 |
|-----|-----|-----|-----|-----|
| + 5 8 | + 1 4 | + 1 7 | + 3 3 | + 3 6 |

| 5 4 | 3 5 | 2 5 | 6 2 | 1 7 |
|-----|-----|-----|-----|-----|
| + 1 7 | + 2 6 | + 2 5 | + 3 8 | + 2 7 |

2. Use a tens and ones chart to add.

| 1 7<br>+ 5 5 | 7 8<br>+ 1 9 | 6 4<br>+ 1 6 | 5 7<br>+ 1 4 | 3 5<br>+ 1 9 |
|---|---|---|---|---|
| 5 6<br>+ 3 8 | 2 4<br>+ 2 6 | 4 3<br>+ 2 9 | 2 7<br>+ 6 4 | 4 8<br>+ 3 8 |
| 4 7<br>+ 1 9 | 1 7<br>+ 4 8 | 3 4<br>+ 1 9 | 3 9<br>+ 3 1 | 5 5<br>+ 2 6 |
| 5 9<br>+ 2 3 | 3 7<br>+ 2 8 | 5 7<br>+ 1 6 | 6 4<br>+ 2 7 | 1 6<br>+ 3 8 |

# Two-Digit Subtraction Without Regrouping

Line up the ones and tens.

First subtract the ones.

| tens | ones |
|------|------|
| 8 | 7 |
| − 4 | 4 |
|  | 3 |

Then subtract the tens.

| tens | ones |
|------|------|
| 8 | 7 |
| − 4 | 4 |
| 4 | 3 |

1. Use a tens and ones chart to subtract. Shade the ones column yellow. Shade the tens column orange.

| 5 8 | 8 7 | 2 9 | 7 4 | 3 3 |
|------|------|------|------|------|
| − 1 1 | − 4 3 | − 1 3 | − 3 0 | − 1 2 |

| 7 8 | 9 6 | 8 4 | 6 7 | 8 5 |
|------|------|------|------|------|
| − 2 3 | − 3 2 | − 7 2 | − 2 3 | − 1 4 |

| 4 9 | 6 7 | 2 5 | 4 6 | 3 6 |
|------|------|------|------|------|
| − 2 7 | − 4 1 | − 1 5 | − 3 5 | − 1 6 |

| 8 6 | 4 3 | 9 8 | 7 2 | 3 3 |
|------|------|------|------|------|
| − 3 1 | − 4 1 | − 2 3 | − 2 1 | − 3 0 |

2. Use a tens and ones chart to subtract.

| | | | | |
|---|---|---|---|---|
| 48<br>− 36 | 67<br>− 40 | 24<br>− 11 | 45<br>− 34 | 36<br>− 12 |
| 89<br>− 32 | 42<br>− 41 | 98<br>− 25 | 76<br>− 34 | 45<br>− 20 |
| 57<br>− 12 | 77<br>− 43 | 28<br>− 14 | 73<br>− 60 | 39<br>− 23 |
| 77<br>− 25 | 95<br>− 31 | 83<br>− 73 | 65<br>− 50 | 85<br>− 22 |

# BRAIN STRETCH

Use ones blocks and tens blocks to subtract 38 − 23.

# Subtraction Match

Draw a line from the question to its matching answer.

| Questions | Answers |
|---|---|
| 45 − 31 | 67 |
| 96 − 52 | 3 |
| 97 − 30 | 31 |
| 28 − 12 | 22 |
| 73 − 22 | 16 |
| 38 − 35 | 14 |
| 79 − 48 | 44 |
| 84 − 62 | 51 |

# Making an Easier Problem

1. Use 10 to make an easier problem. Then subtract.

12 – 9 =

12 – 9 = **13** – 10 = **3**
I know 9 + 1 = 10.
So, I add 1 to each number.
Then I subtract.

14 – 8 =

14 – 8 = ___ – 10 = ___

Add 2 to each number.

13 – 9 =

13 – 9 = ___ – 10 = ___

Add ___ to each number.

15 – 7 =

15 – 7 = ___ – 10 = ___

Add ___ to each number.

16 – 7 =

16 – 7 = ___ – 10 = ___

Add ___ to each number.

17 – 6 =

17 – 6 = ___ – ___ = ___

Add ___ to each number.

19 – 6 =

19 – 6 = ___ – 10 = ___

Add ___ to each number.

18 – 7 =

18 – 7 = ___ – ___ = ___

Add ___ to each number.

2. Use 10 to make an easier problem. Then subtract.

---

$23 - 18 =$

$23 - 18 = \underline{\textbf{25}} - 20 = \underline{\textbf{5}}$
I know $18 + 2 = 20$.
So, I add 2 to each number.
Then I subtract.

---

$34 - 19 =$

$34 - 19 = \underline{\quad} - 20 = \underline{\quad}$

Add 1 to each number.

---

$22 - 16 =$

$22 - 16 = \underline{\quad} - 20 = \underline{\quad}$

Add $\underline{\quad}$ to each number.

---

$29 - 17 =$

$29 - 17 = \underline{\quad} - \underline{\quad} = \underline{\quad}$

Add $\underline{\quad}$ to each number.

---

$28 - 19 =$

$28 - 19 = \underline{\quad} - 20 = \underline{\quad}$

Add $\underline{\quad}$ to each number.

---

$42 - 18 =$

$42 - 18 = \underline{\quad} - \underline{\quad} = \underline{\quad}$

Add $\underline{\quad}$ to each number.

---

$31 - 16 =$

$31 - 16 = \underline{\quad} - 20 = \underline{\quad}$

Add $\underline{\quad}$ to each number.

---

$34 - 19 =$

$34 - 19 = \underline{\quad} - \underline{\quad} = \underline{\quad}$

Add $\underline{\quad}$ to each number.

# Two-Digit Subtraction with Regrouping

Line up the ones and the tens.
Subtract the ones.
Trade 1 ten from the tens for 10 ones in the ones.
Write the ones.
Then write the tens.

You cannot take 9 from 2. So, trade 1 ten from the tens for 10 ones. Now there are 12 ones.

1. Use a tens and ones chart to subtract. Shade the ones column yellow. Shade the tens column orange.

| 61 | 73 | 61 | 42 | 24 |
| --- | --- | --- | --- | --- |
| − 25 | − 16 | − 24 | − 33 | − 17 |

| 35 | 52 | 71 | 63 | 31 |
| --- | --- | --- | --- | --- |
| − 18 | − 25 | − 54 | − 27 | − 12 |

| 54 | 83 | 92 | 71 | 40 |
| --- | --- | --- | --- | --- |
| − 46 | − 26 | − 75 | − 13 | − 29 |

# Two-Digit Subtraction with Regrouping

2. Use a tens and ones chart to subtract.
   You will need to regroup.

|  |  |  |  |  |
|---|---|---|---|---|
| 3 4<br>− 2 7 | 5 1<br>− 3 3 | 7 0<br>− 5 4 | 6 2<br>− 1 6 | 3 0<br>− 1 1 |
| 5 2<br>− 3 9 | 6 7<br>− 4 8 | 4 1<br>− 3 4 | 9 2<br>− 5 6 | 4 2<br>− 2 4 |
| 5 3<br>− 4 5 | 8 2<br>− 3 7 | 9 1<br>− 7 6 | 8 0<br>− 1 9 | 3 7<br>− 1 8 |
| 6 0<br>− 2 4 | 7 2<br>− 2 5 | 5 0<br>− 2 3 | 4 1<br>− 3 2 | 3 1<br>− 1 6 |

# Subtraction Riddle

Solve the math riddle.

| | | | |
|---|---|---|---|
| 40 **E**<br>− 33 | 31 **P**<br>− 19 | 54 **H**<br>− 25 | 77 **N**<br>− 39 |
| 96 **U**<br>− 38 | 95 **W**<br>− 79 | 51 **O**<br>− 38 | 62 **T**<br>− 15 |
| 91 **S**<br>− 22 | 24 **Z**<br>− 19 | 73 **M**<br>− 29 | 44 **I**<br>− 19 |

Watch out! Some letters are not used in the riddle.

16  29   7  38 | 69  13  44   7  13  38   7 | 69  47   7  12  69 |

13  38 | 25  47  69 | 44  13  58  69   7   **!**

# Word Problems

Decide if you need to add or subtract. Underline any words that help you decide. Then solve the problem. Show your work. Circle Add or Subtract.

1. Paul has 23 blue marbles and 39 red marbles. How many marbles are there altogether?

   There are _________ marbles.

   Add

   Subtract

2. There were 41 birds in the tree. 23 birds flew away. How many birds are left in the tree?

   _________ birds are left.

   Add

   Subtract

3. There were 82 jelly beans in the jar. David ate 36 of them. How many jelly beans are left?

   There are _________ jelly beans left.

   Add

   Subtract

4. Rama has 38 green buttons and 28 blue buttons. How many buttons does she have in all?

   There are _________ buttons in all.

   Add

   Subtract

# Introducing Multiplication

1. Write the addition sentence and the multiplication sentence.

Look at the groups of 3.

|  | Addition Sentence | Multiplication Sentence |
| --- | --- | --- |
|  | There are 3 equal groups. | There are 3 groups of 3. |
|  | 3 + 3 + 3 = **9** | 3 × 3 = **9** |

6 + 6 = _____     2 × 6 = _____

2 + 2 + 2 = _____     3 × 2 = _____

10 + 10 =      2 × 10 = _____

3 + 3 + 3 + 3 = _____     4 × 3 = _____

7 + 7 = _____     2 × 7 = _____

8 + 8 = _____     2 × 8 =

2. Write the addition sentence and the multiplication sentence.

___ + ___ + ___ = ___          ___ × ___ = ___

___ + ___ = ___          ___ × ___ = ___

___ + ___ = ___          ___ × ___ = ___

___ + ___ + ___ + ___ = ___          ___ × ___ = ___

___ + ___ = ___          ___ × ___ = ___

___ + ___ + ___ = ___          ___ × ___ = ___

___ + ___ + ___ = ___          ___ × ___ = ___

___ + ___ = ___          ___ × ___ = ___

___ + ___ + ___ + ___ = ___          ___ × ___ = ___

# Skip Counting

Fill in the missing numbers.

1. Count by 2s.

There are __________ groups of two creatures.    There are __________ creatures altogether.

2. Count by 5s.

There are __________ groups of five creatures.    There are __________ creatures altogether.

3. Count by 10s.

There are __________ groups of ten creatures.    There are __________ creatures altogether.

# Fractions: Equal Parts

There are two equal parts.
Each part is one half.

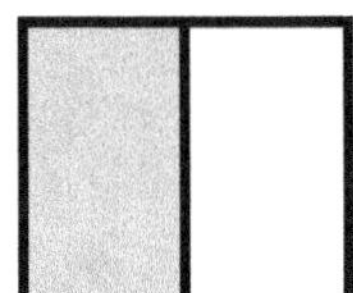

$\frac{1}{2}$ means that 1 out of 2 equal parts is shaded.

**Which shapes show 2 equal parts? Shade one half.**

1. 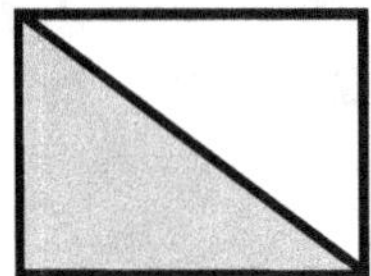

2. 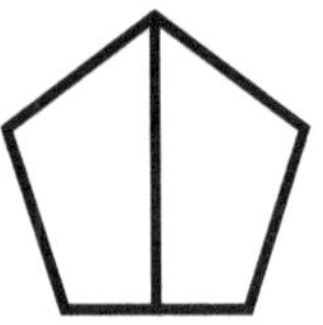 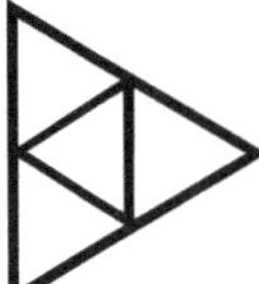 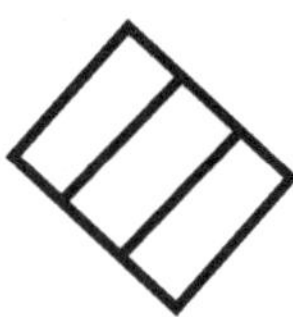

3. 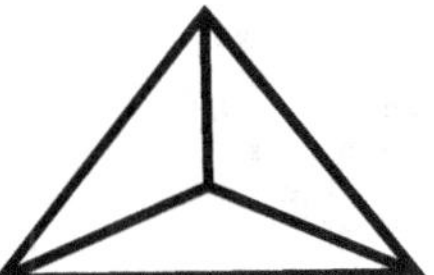  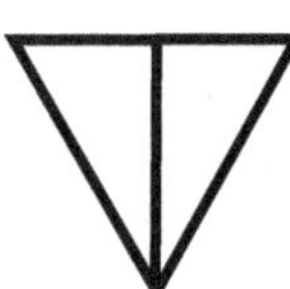

4.   

5. 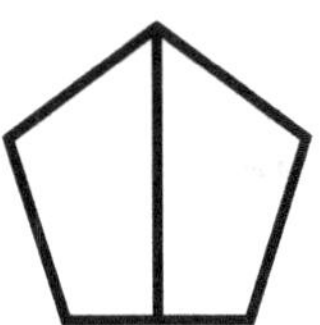  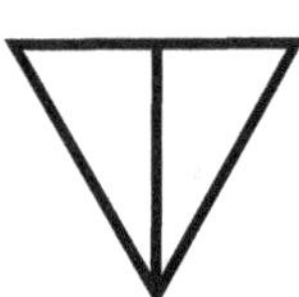

6.  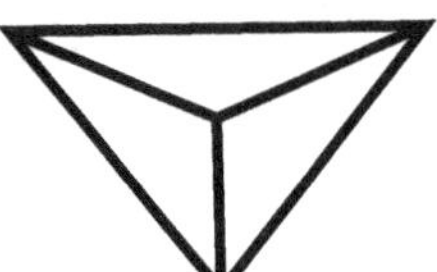 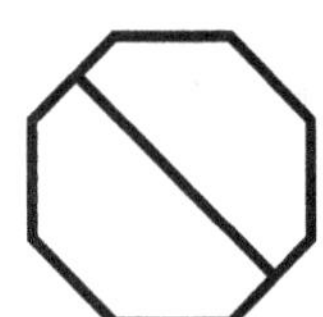

 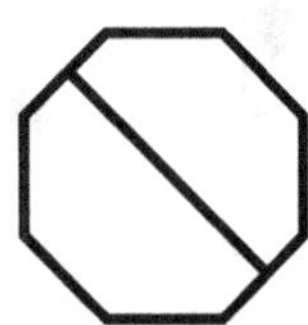

# Exploring Fractions

There are 3 equal parts.  $\frac{1}{3}$ means that 1 out of 3 equal parts is shaded.

1. What fraction is shaded? Circle the fraction.

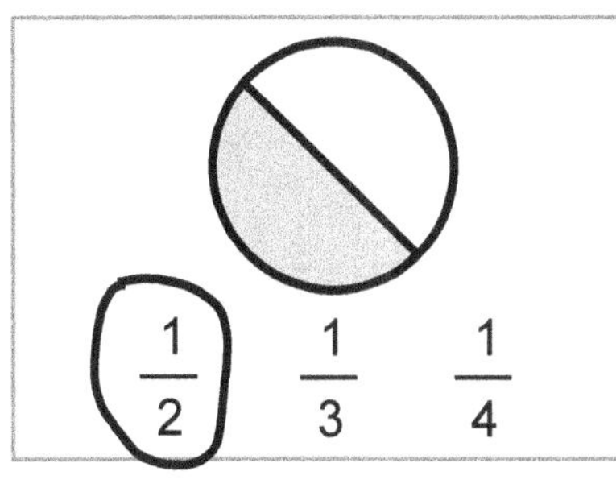

$\frac{1}{2}$    $\frac{1}{3}$    $\frac{1}{4}$

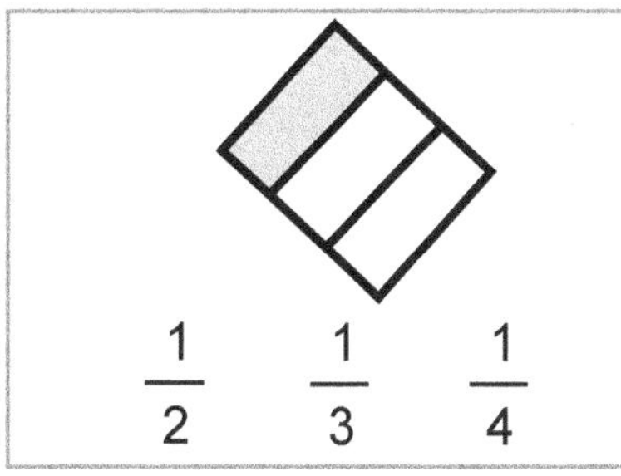

$\frac{1}{2}$    $\frac{1}{3}$    $\frac{1}{4}$

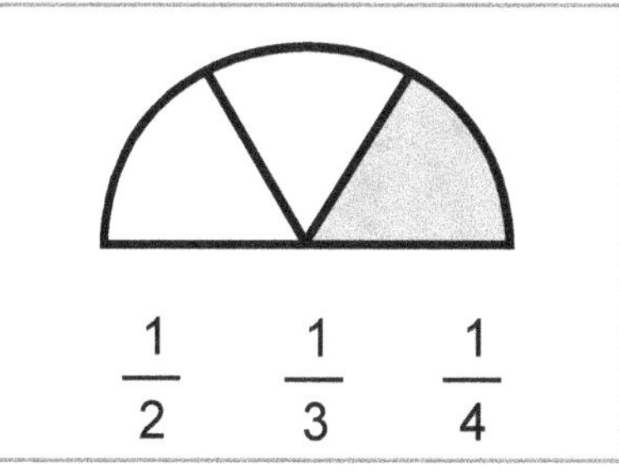

$\frac{1}{2}$    $\frac{1}{3}$    $\frac{1}{4}$

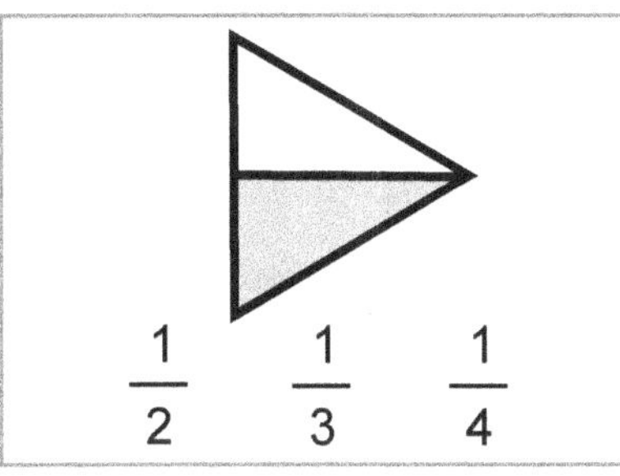

$\frac{1}{2}$    $\frac{1}{3}$    $\frac{1}{4}$

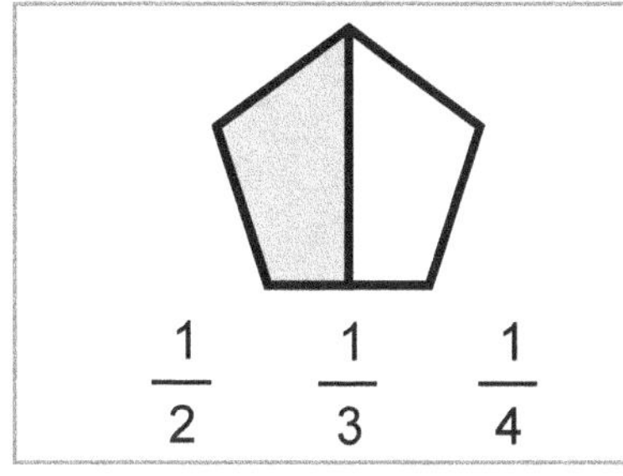

$\frac{1}{2}$    $\frac{1}{3}$    $\frac{1}{4}$

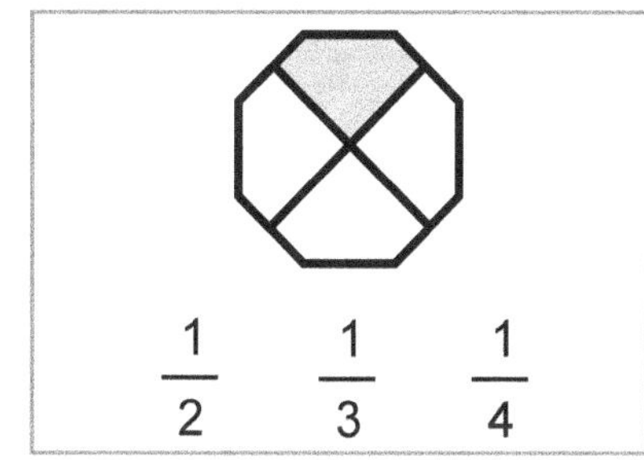

$\frac{1}{2}$    $\frac{1}{3}$    $\frac{1}{4}$

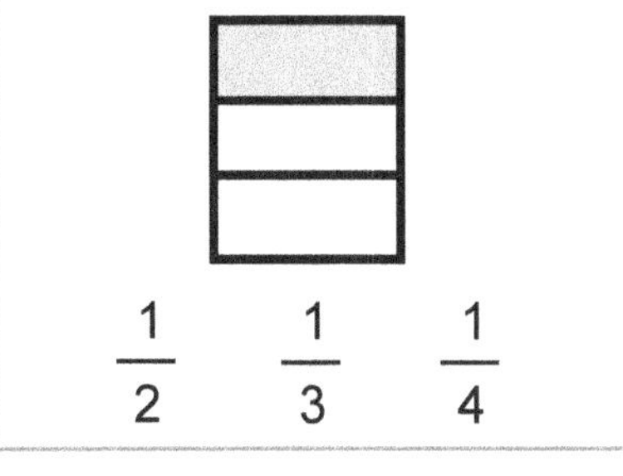

$\frac{1}{2}$    $\frac{1}{3}$    $\frac{1}{4}$

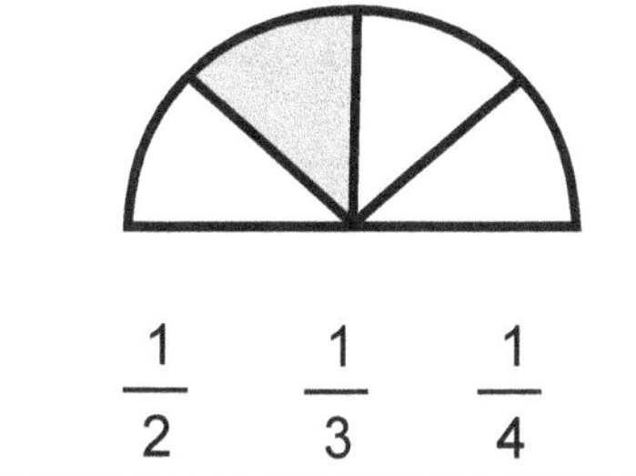

$\frac{1}{2}$    $\frac{1}{3}$    $\frac{1}{4}$

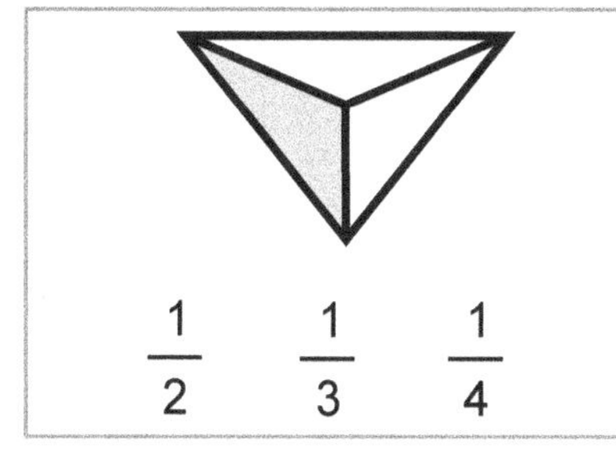

$\frac{1}{2}$    $\frac{1}{3}$    $\frac{1}{4}$

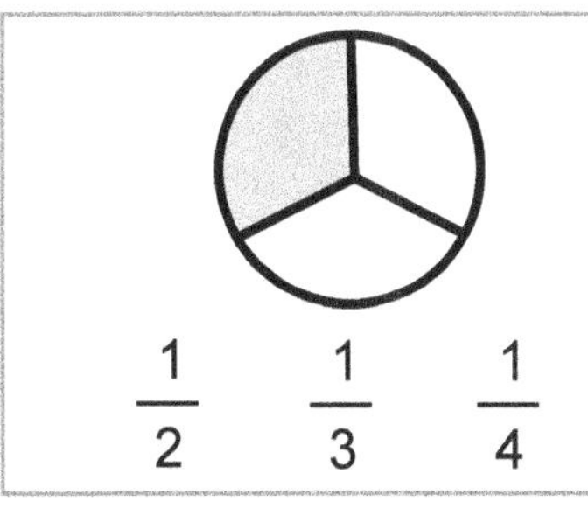

$\frac{1}{2}$    $\frac{1}{3}$    $\frac{1}{4}$

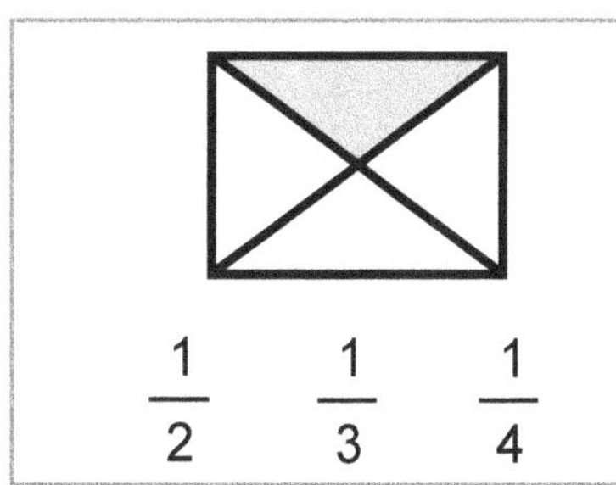

$\frac{1}{2}$    $\frac{1}{3}$    $\frac{1}{4}$

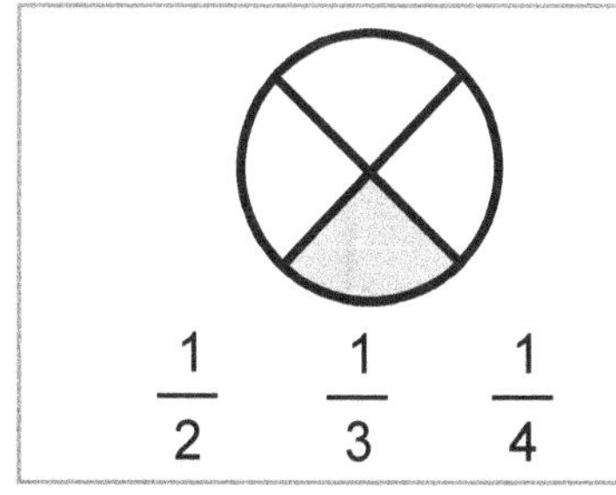

$\frac{1}{2}$    $\frac{1}{3}$    $\frac{1}{4}$

2.  What fraction is shaded? Write the fraction.

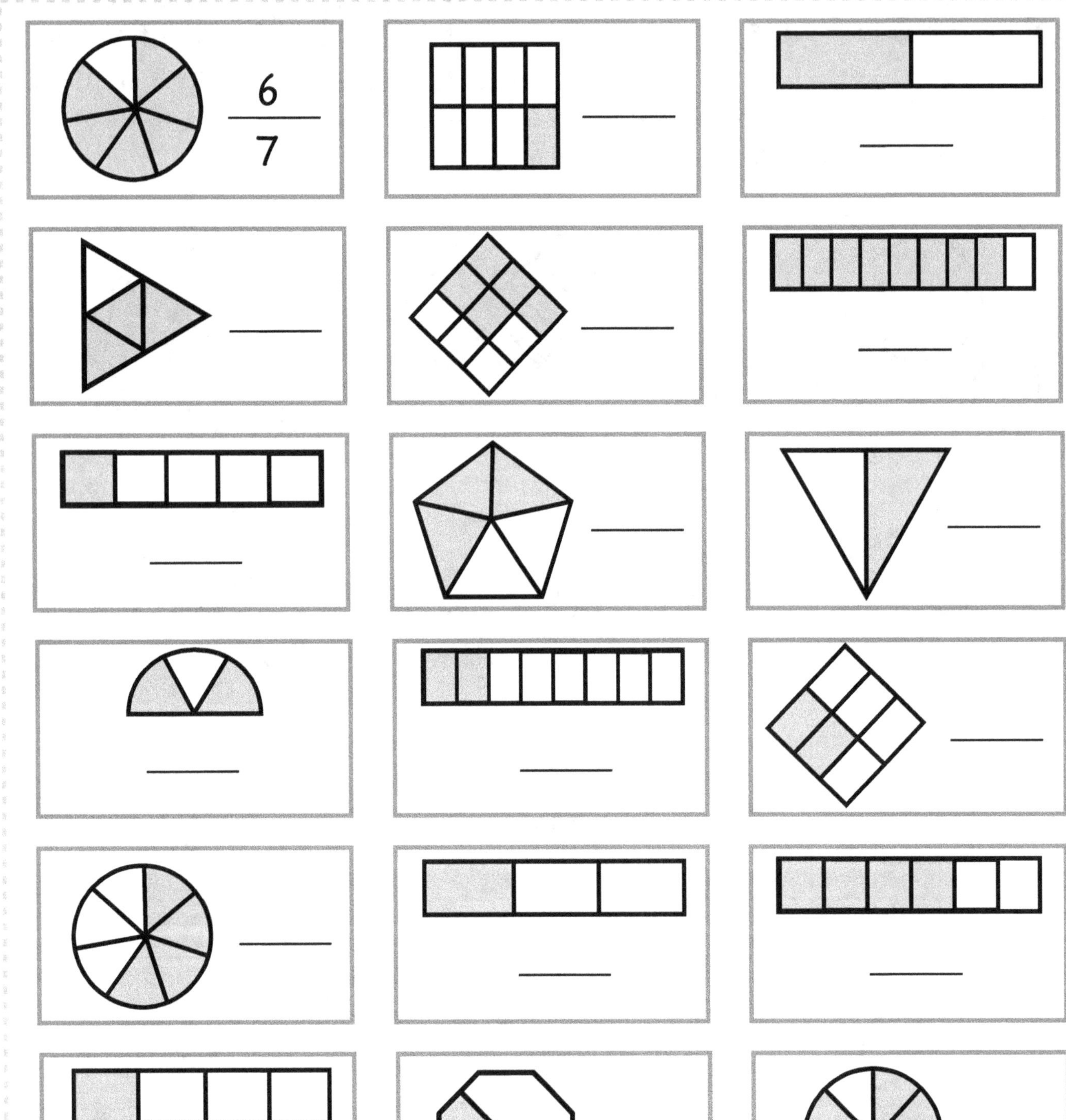

# Coloring Fractions

Color the fractions.

Color $\frac{1}{4}$ blue.
Color $\frac{1}{4}$ green.
Color $\frac{1}{4}$ red.
Color $\frac{1}{4}$ yellow.

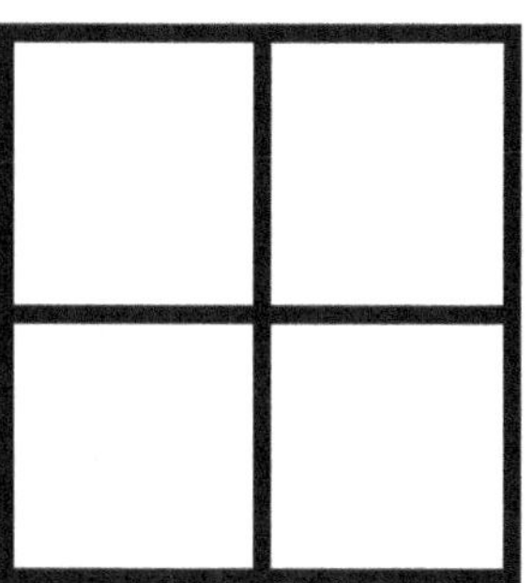

Color $\frac{1}{2}$ blue.
Color $\frac{1}{2}$ green.

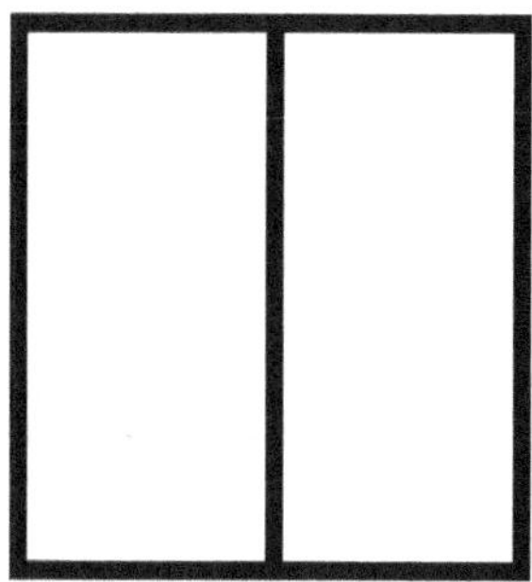

Color $\frac{1}{4}$ blue.
Color $\frac{1}{4}$ green.
Color $\frac{2}{4}$ red.

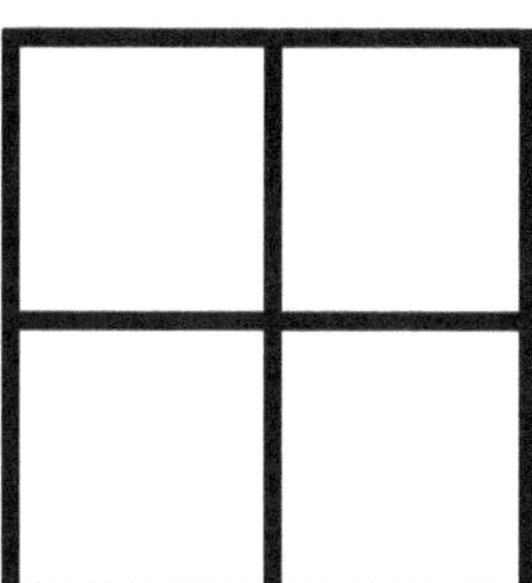

Color $\frac{1}{2}$ blue.
Color $\frac{1}{2}$ green.

Color $\frac{1}{3}$ blue.
Color $\frac{2}{3}$ green.

Color $\frac{1}{3}$ blue.
Color $\frac{1}{3}$ green.
Color $\frac{1}{3}$ red.

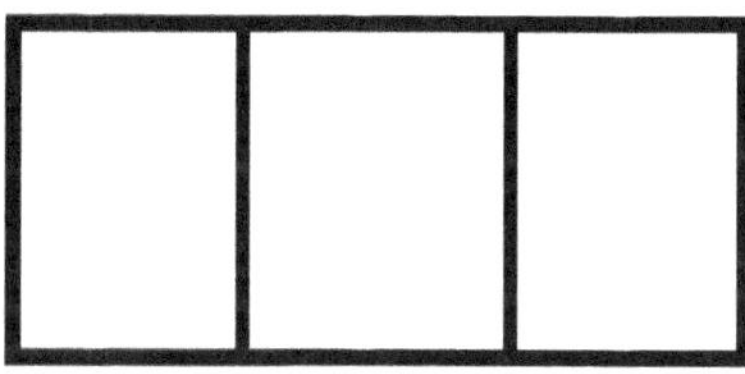

## BRAIN STRETCH

Color your own fractions.

 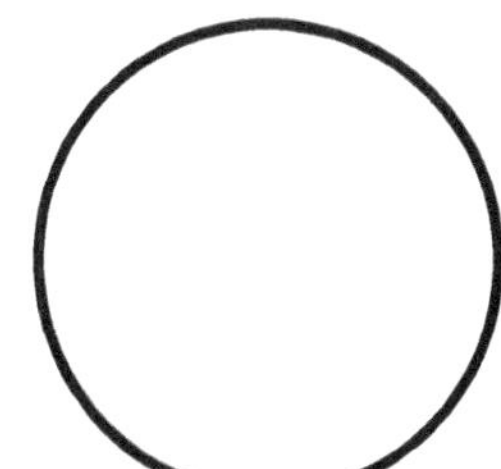 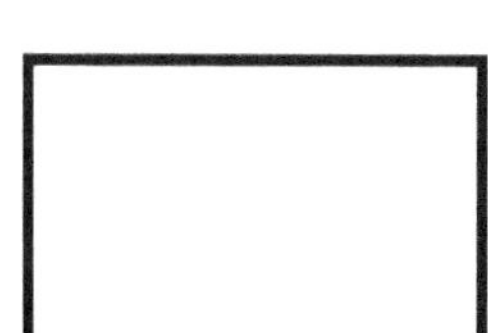 

# Fractions as Part of a Group

Color the fraction.

Color $\frac{1}{4}$ .

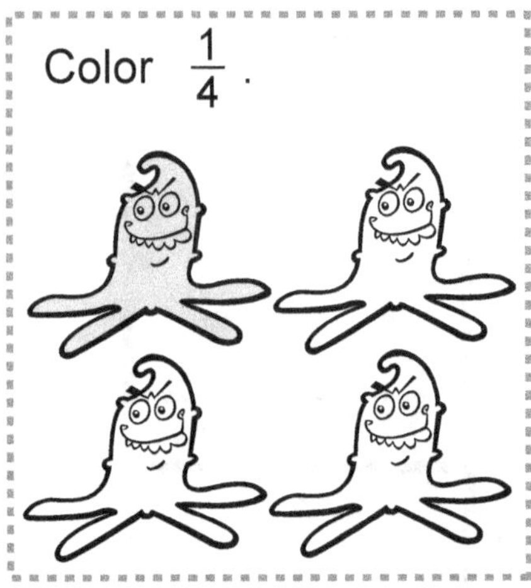

Color $\frac{1}{2}$ .

Color $\frac{2}{4}$ .

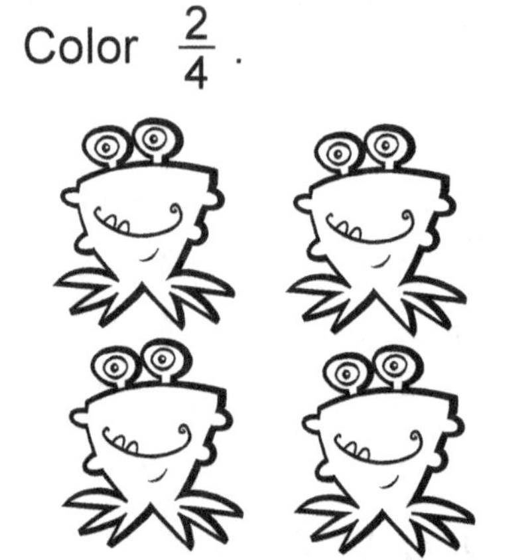

Color $\frac{1}{3}$ .

Color $\frac{1}{2}$ .

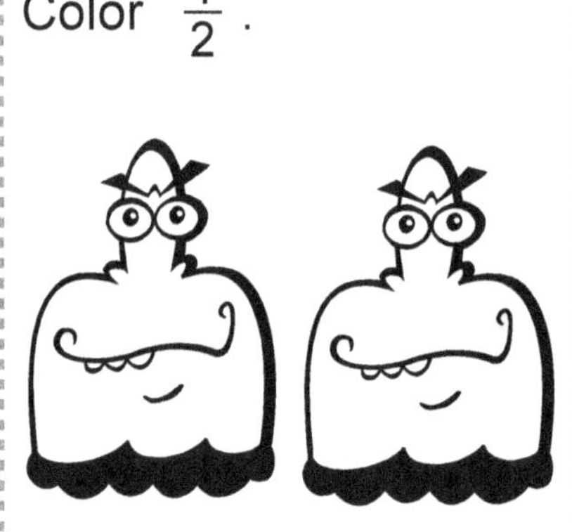

Color $\frac{2}{3}$ .

Color $\frac{3}{4}$ .

Color $\frac{1}{3}$ .

Color $\frac{1}{2}$ .

# Fraction Problems

Draw a picture and show the answer as a fraction.

1. Alex cut a pizza into 4 equal slices. He ate 1 slice. What fraction of the pizza did he eat?

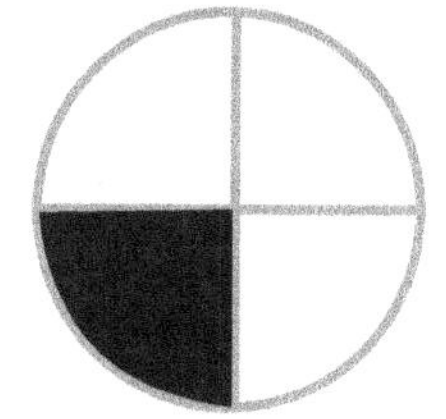

_______

2. Margaux counts 4 mailboxes on her street. 3 are green. What fraction of the mailboxes are green?

_______

3. Katie has 3 books from the library. She read 2 of them. What fraction of the books did she read?

_______

4. Madelyn has 4 carrot sticks for a snack. She put cheese on 2 of them. What fraction of the carrots have cheese?

_______

5. Ivan has 2 health bars. He gave 1 bar to his friend. What fraction of the health bars did he give away?

_______

# Telling Time to the Hour

Write the time in two ways. Highlight the hour hand in blue.

On a clock, the **hour hand** is short.

You can write the time in two ways.
It is **2 o'clock** or **2:00**.

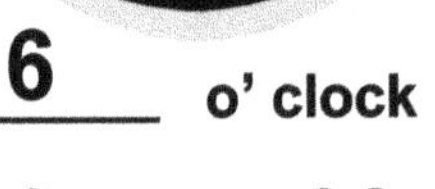

**6** _____ o' clock

**6** : **00**

_____ o' clock

___ : ___

_____ o' clock

___ : ___

_____ o' clock

___ : ___

_____ o' clock

___ : ___

_____ o' clock

___ : ___

_____ o' clock

___ : ___

_____ o' clock

___ : ___

# Telling Time to the Half Hour

Write the time in two ways.
Highlight the hour hand blue. Highlight the minute hand red.

The **minute hand** points to 6.
The **hour hand** is after 3 but before 4.

It is **3:30** or **half past 3.**

half past __**8**__

__**8**__ : __**30**__

half past __________

______ : ______

half past __________

______ : ______

half past __________

______ : ______

half past __________

______ : ______

half past __________

______ : ______

half past __________

______ : ______

half past __________

______ : ______

# Telling Time to Quarter Past the Hour

Write the time two ways.
Highlight the hour hand blue. Highlight the minute hand red.

The **minute hand** points to 3.
The **hour hand** is just after 8.

It is quarter past **8** or **8:15**.

quarter past ___12___

__12__ : __15__

quarter past _______

____ : ____

quarter past _______

____ : ____

quarter past _______

____ : ____

quarter past _______

____ : ____

quarter past _______

____ : ____

quarter past _______

____ : ____

quarter past _______

____ : ____

# Telling Time to the Quarter Hour

Write the time in two ways.
Highlight the hour hand blue. Highlight the minute hand red.

The **minute hand** points to 9.
The **hour hand** is after 7 and close to 8.

It is **quarter to 8** or **7:45**.

quarter to _____**1**_____

___**12**___ : ___**45**___

quarter to _________

_______ : _______

quarter to _________

_______ : _______

quarter to _________

_______ : _______

quarter to _________

_______ : _______

quarter to _________

_______ : _______

quarter to _________

_______ : _______

quarter to _________

_______ : _______

# What Time Is It?

Circle the correct time.
Highlight the hour hand blue. Highlight the minute hand red.

4:00 or 4:30

7:00  or  7:30

8:00  or  8:30

11:00  or  11:30

3:00  or  3:30

3:00  or  3:30

10:00  or  10:30

5:00  or  5:30

12:00  or  12:30

9:00  or  9:30

4:00  or  4:30

2:00  or  2:30

# Showing the Time

Draw the two hands on the clock to show the time.
Highlight the hour hand blue. Highlight the minute hand red.

2:15

8:00

10:30

4:45

11:30

12:45

9:30

4:15

6:00

7:45

9:00

1:30

# Calendar Time

1. Write the months of the year in order.

_______________________

_______________________

_______________________

_______________________

_______________________

_______________________

_______________________

_______________________

_______________________

_______________________

_______________________

_______________________

May

September

December

February

August

April

July

March

October

June

November

January

2. How many months in a year? _______________________

# Reading a Calendar

Use the calendar to answer the questions.

## April

| Sunday | Monday | Tuesday | Wednesday | Thursday | Friday | Saturday |
| --- | --- | --- | --- | --- | --- | --- |
|  |  | 1 | 2 | 3 | 4 | 5 |
| 6 | 7 | 8 | 9 | 10 | 11 | 12 |
| 13 | 14 | 15 | 16 | 17 | 18 | 19 |
| 20 | 21 | 22 | 23 | 24 | 25 | 26 |
| 27 | 28 | 29 | 30 |  |  |  |

1. What day of the week is April 10?

2. How many Tuesdays are there?

3. How many Saturdays are there?

4. What is the date of the first Monday?

## December

| Sunday | Monday | Tuesday | Wednesday | Thursday | Friday | Saturday |
| --- | --- | --- | --- | --- | --- | --- |
|  |  |  |  | 1 | 2 | 3 |
| 4 | 5 | 6 | 7 | 8 | 9 | 10 |
| 11 | 12 | 13 | 14 | 15 | 16 | 17 |
| 18 | 19 | 20 | 21 | 22 | 23 | 24 |
| 25 | 26 | 27 | 28 | 29 | 30 | 31 |

5. How many days are there in the month?

6. What day of the week is December 12?

7. On what day of the week will next month begin?

8. How many Fridays are there?

# Getting to Know Coins

1. Draw a line from the coin to its value.

This is a penny.

25¢

This is a nickel.

5¢

This is a dime.

100¢

This is a quarter.

50¢

This is a half dollar.

10¢

This is a dollar.

1¢

2. Write the value of the coin in cents. Then write the name of the coin. Use the money words.

**penny**   **nickel**   **dime**   **quarter**   **half dollar**   **dollar**

| Coin | Value | Name |
|---|---|---|
| Quarter Dollar | __________ ¢ | |
| One Dime | __________ ¢ | |
| One Cent | __________ ¢ | |
| Half Dollar | __________ ¢ | |
| Five Cents | __________ ¢ | |
| $1 Dollar | __________ ¢ | |

3. Circle the dollars in red. Circle the quarters in green. Circle the dimes in blue. Circle the nickels in yellow. Circle the half dollars in orange. Circle the pennies in purple.

# BRAIN STRETCH

How many dimes? __________     How many dollars? __________

How many nickels? __________     How many quarters? __________

How many half dollars? __________     How many pennies? __________

# Estimating

Estimate the amount of money. Use blue to circle groups of 25¢.
Count the money. Use red to circle groups of 10¢. Then count the money.

**Mary**

Estimate ___90___ ¢  Count _25_¢ _50_¢ _60_¢ _70_¢ _80_¢ _90_¢ _95_¢

**Dan**

Estimate ________ ¢  Count _____¢ _____¢ _____¢ _____¢ _____¢ _____¢

**Tessa**

Estimate ________ ¢  Count _____¢ _____¢ _____¢ _____¢ _____¢

**John**

Estimate ________ ¢  Count _____¢ _____¢ _____¢ _____¢ _____¢

# Counting Dimes and Nickels

Find the value of the coins. Count by 10s for dimes. Count by 5s for nickels.

10 ¢  20 ¢  30 ¢  40 ¢  45 ¢  50 ¢ = 50 ¢

_____ ¢ _____ ¢ _____ ¢ _____ ¢ _____ ¢ = _________ ¢

_____ ¢ _____ ¢ _____ ¢ _____ ¢ = _________ ¢

_____ ¢ _____ ¢ _____ ¢ _____ ¢ = _________ ¢

_____ ¢ _____ ¢ _____ ¢ _____ ¢ _____ ¢ _____ ¢ = _________ ¢

# How Much Money?

1. Calculate how much money each person has.

Spencer       Total

25¢     25¢     10¢     10¢     5¢     <u>0.75</u>¢

Ben      

_____¢   _____¢   _____¢   _____¢   _____¢    _____¢

Carrie      

_____¢   _____¢   _____¢   _____¢   _____¢    _____¢

Tanya      

_____¢   _____¢   _____¢   _____¢   _____¢    _____¢

2. Who has the most money? _______________________________

3. Who has the least money? _______________________________

4. Calculate how much money each person has.

Jane      

______ ¢  ______ ¢  ______ ¢  ______ ¢  ______ ¢    Total ______ ¢

Suzanne      

______ ¢  ______ ¢  ______ ¢  ______ ¢  ______ ¢    ______ ¢

Omar      

______ ¢  ______ ¢  ______ ¢  ______ ¢  ______ ¢    ______ ¢

James      

______ ¢  ______ ¢  ______ ¢  ______ ¢  ______ ¢    ______ ¢

5. Who has the most money? ________________________________

6. Who has the least money? ________________________________

# Trading Coins

Count the money. Make each amount using the fewest coins. Draw the coins.

Coin value ______________

Coin value ______________

Coin value ______________

Coin value ______________

Coin value ______________

# Money Match

Match the cost of each item with the coins.

95 cents

1 dollar

40 cents

50 cents

60 cents

# Missing Coins

Complete the number sentence. Then draw the missing coins.

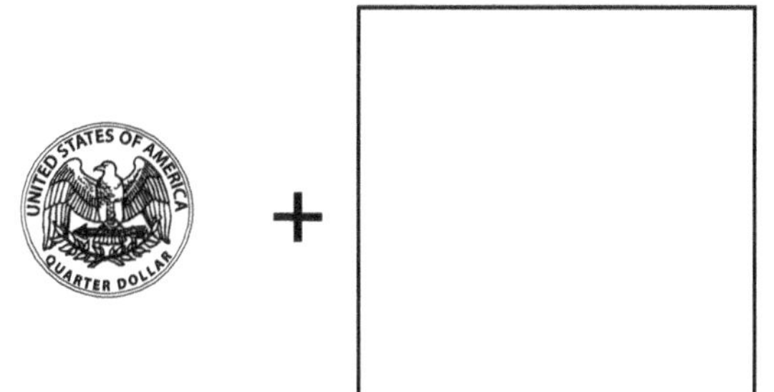 +

25¢  +  _____  =  30¢

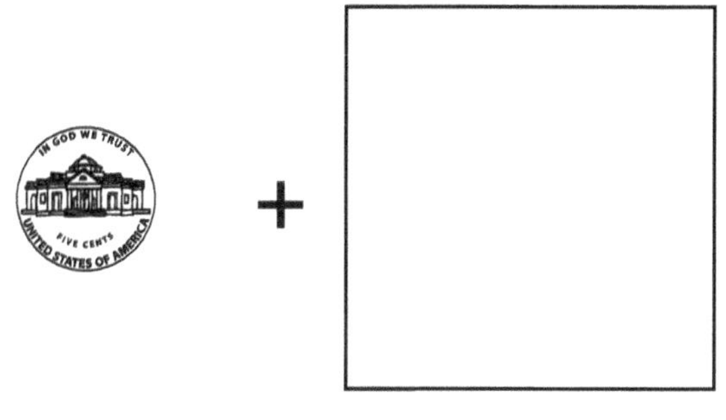 +

5¢  +  _____  =  50¢

 +

40¢  +  _____  =  80¢

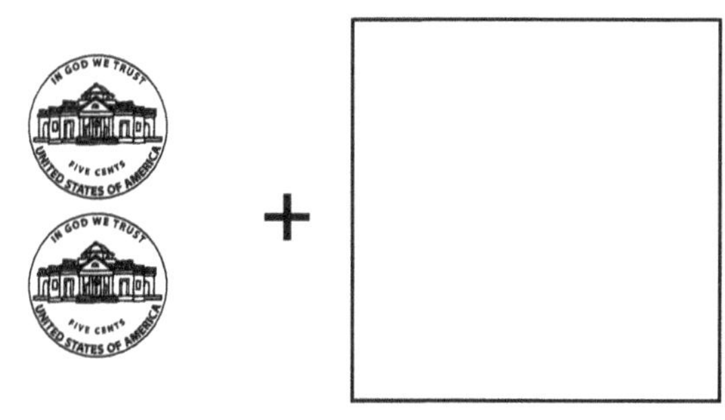 +

10¢  +  _____  =  65¢

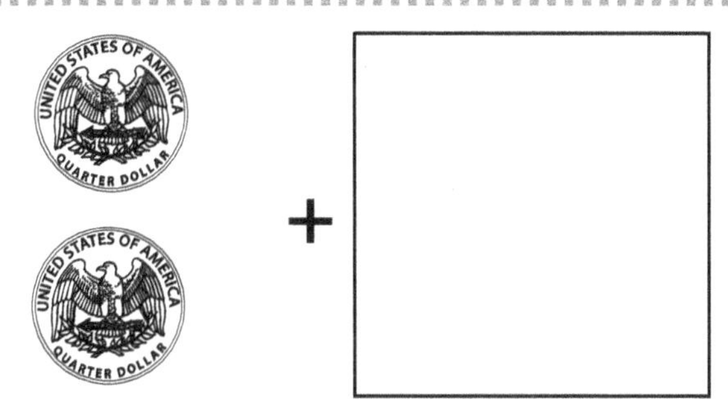 +

50¢  +  _____  =  $1.00

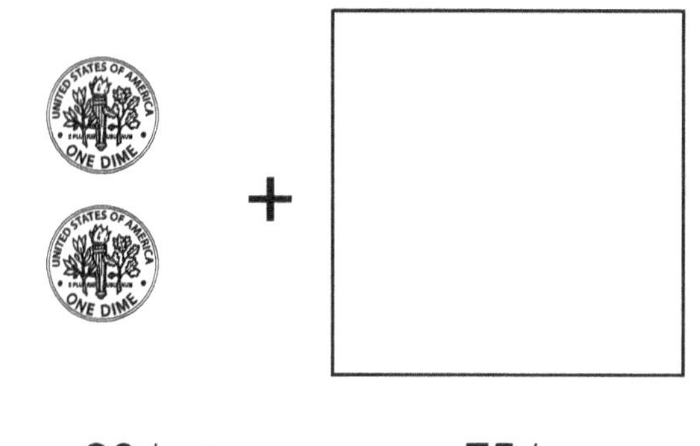 +

20¢  +  _____  =  75¢

# Equal Amounts

Show 2 different ways to make the same amount. Draw the coins.

| | First Way | Second Way |
| --- | --- | --- |
| 35¢ | | |
| 80¢ | | |
| 50¢ | | |
| $1.00 | | |

# Exploring Length Using Non-standard Units

1. How long is each object in ⬭ ?

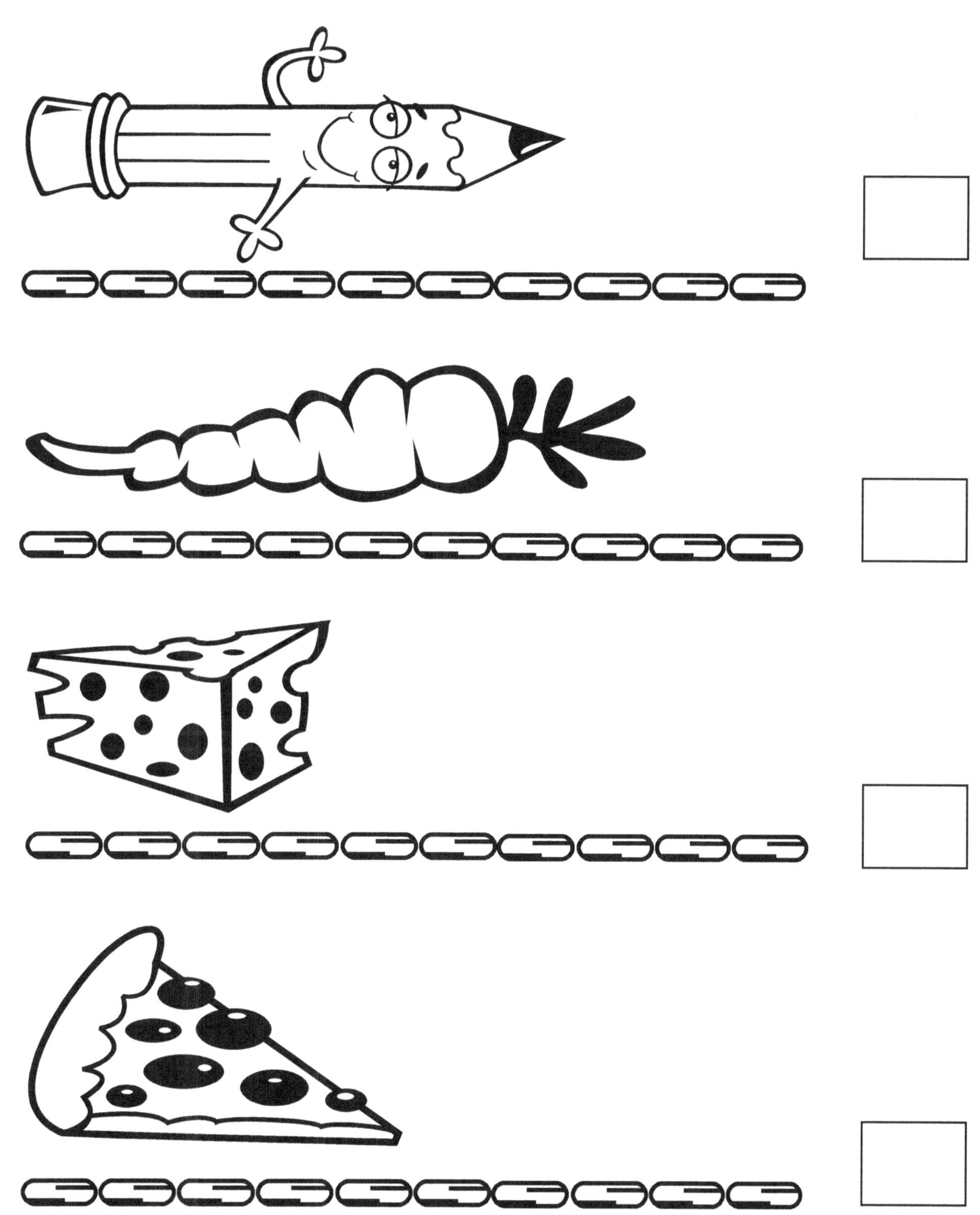

# Exploring Length In Centimetres

1. Write the length in centimetres. Write **cm** for centimetres.

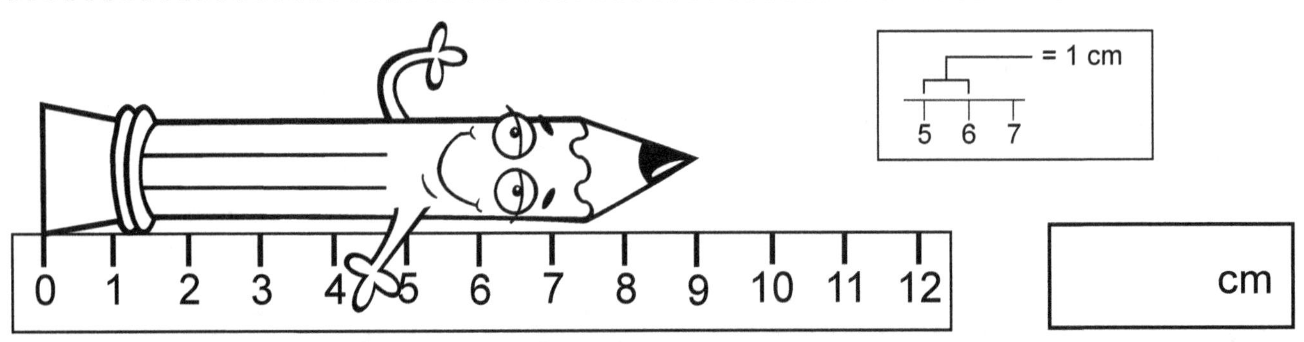


cm

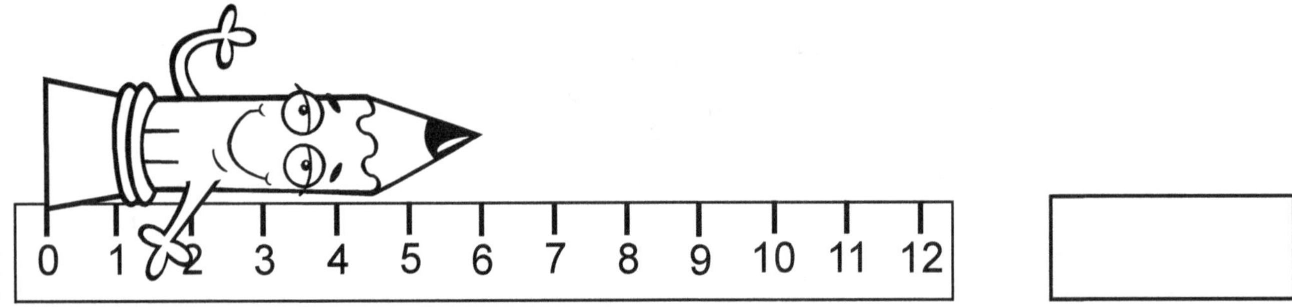


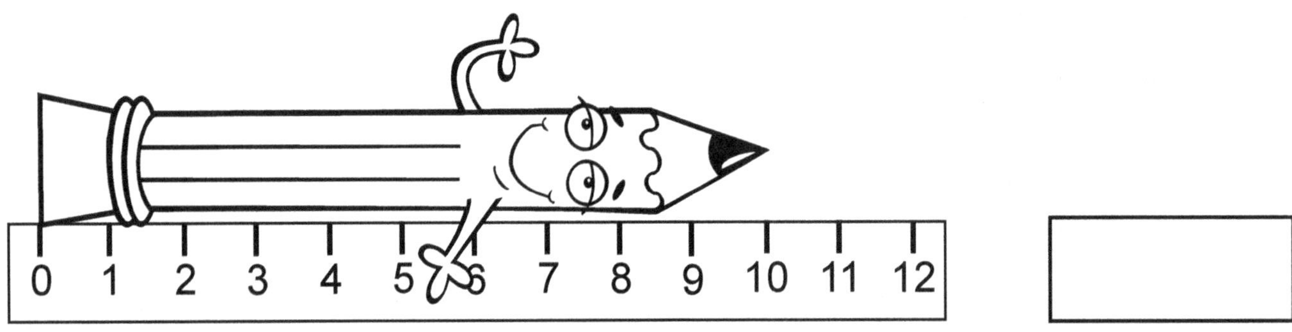


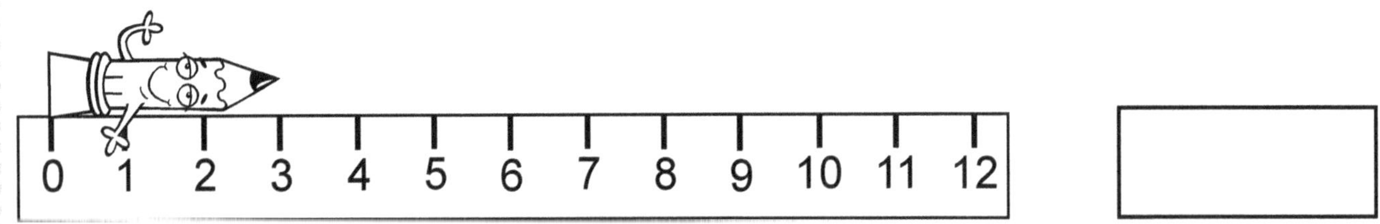

2. Write the length in centimetres. Use cm.

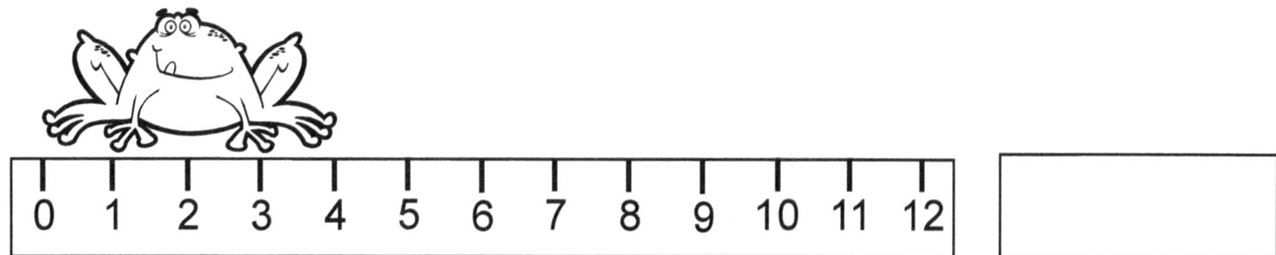

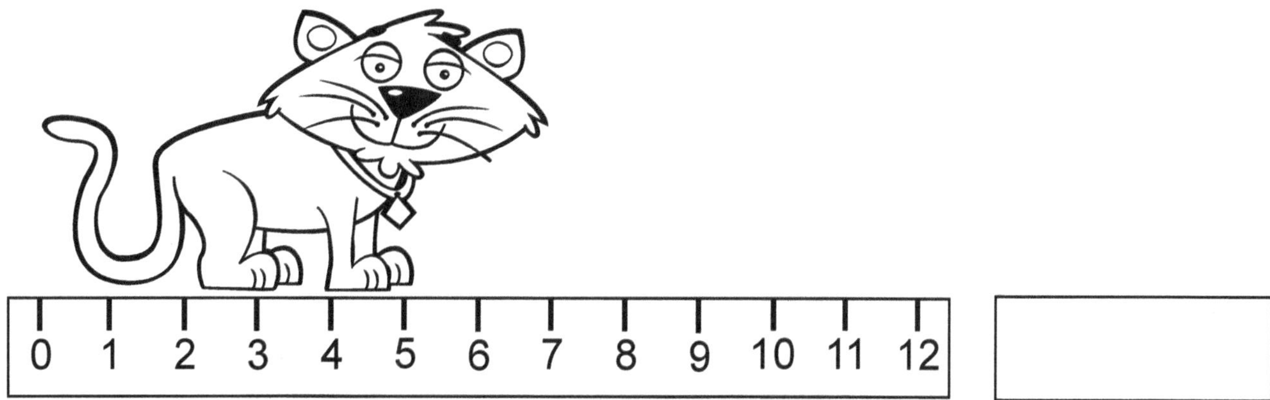

## BRAIN STRETCH

About how many cubes long is
the caterpillar? Circle the answer.

about 2 cubes

about 4 cubes

about 6 cubes

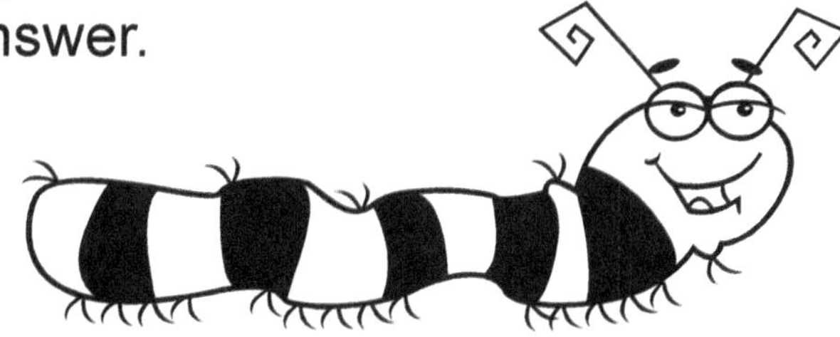

# Exploring Mass

Mass measures how much something weighs.

What is the mass of the creature? Count the blocks to find out.

______ blocks

______ blocks

______ blocks

______ blocks

______ blocks

______ blocks

______ blocks

______ blocks

______ blocks

# Exploring Capacity

Capacity is the amount that something can hold.

In each question, color the container that holds more.

# Exploring Measurement

Draw a line from the activity to the measurement tool you would use.

You need to measure a cup of flour to make bread.

You want to know the temperature.

You want to measure the length of your book.

You want to weigh some apples.

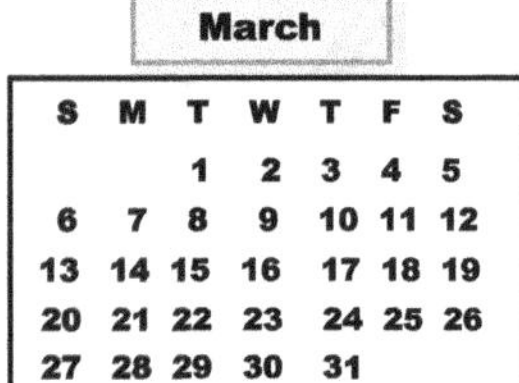



You want to know what time it is.

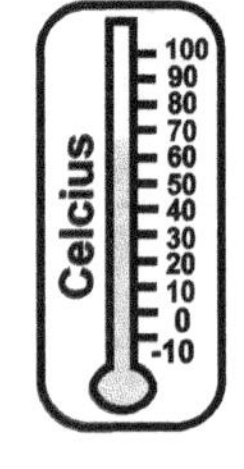



You want to know the date.

# Exploring Perimeter

To find the perimeter (distance around), add the lengths of the sides.

5 units + 5 units + 3 units + 3 units = 16 units

The perimeter is 16 units.

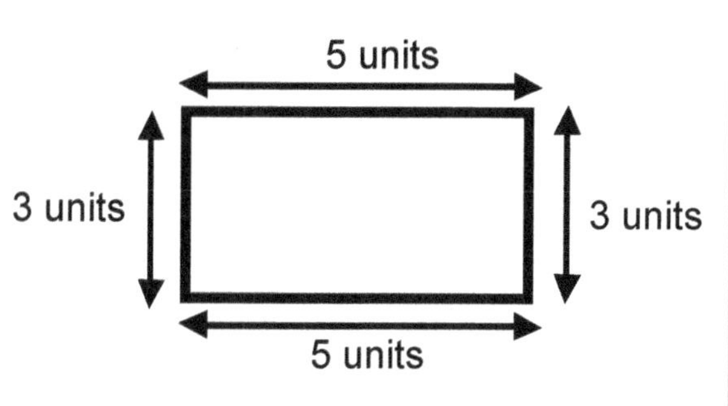


What is the perimeter of each shape?

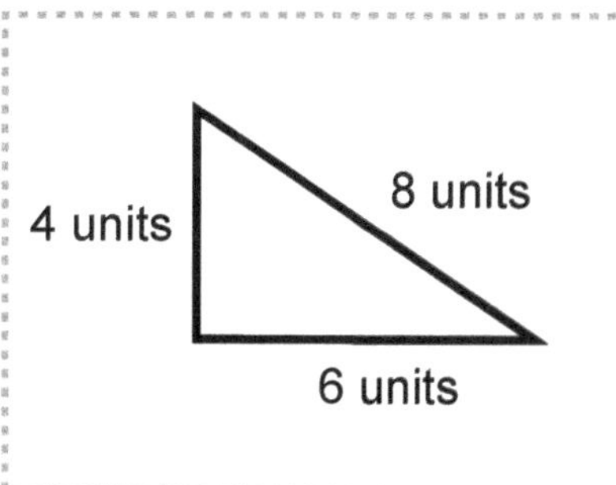


___ + ___ + ___ = ___ units

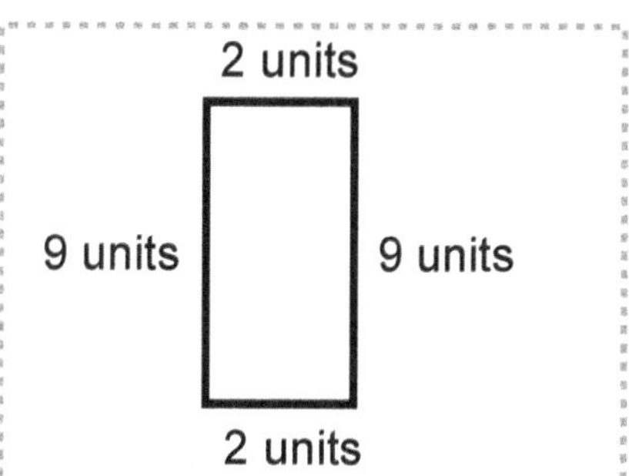


___ + ___ + ___ + ___ = ___ units

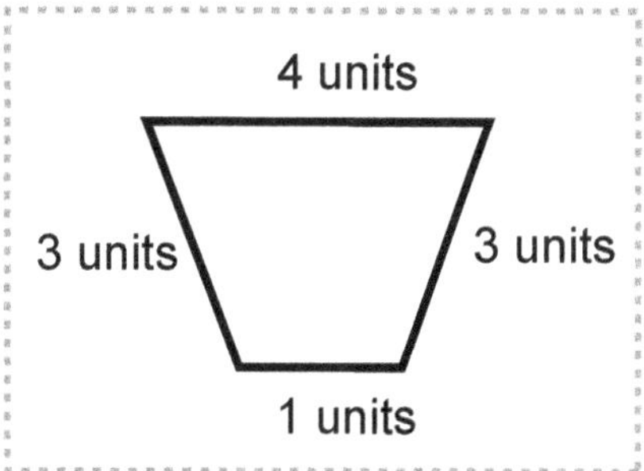


___ + ___ + ___ + ___ = ___ units

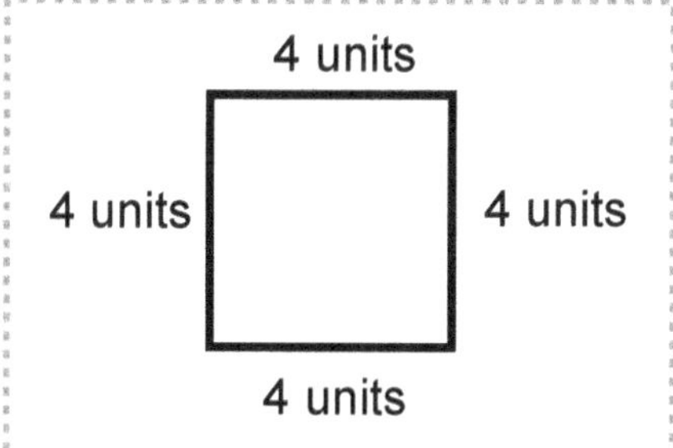


___ + ___ + ___ + ___ = ___ units

# Exploring Area

Area is the number of units that cover a figure.

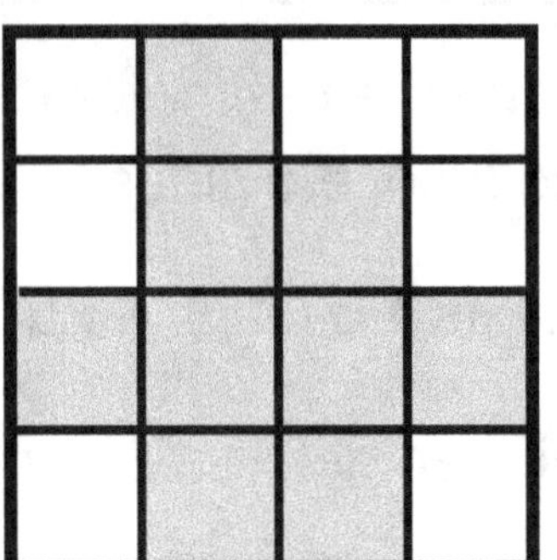

1 square is 1 unit.

Count the number of square units that cover the figure.

The area of the shaded figure is 9 square units.

Find the area by counting the squares that cover the figure.

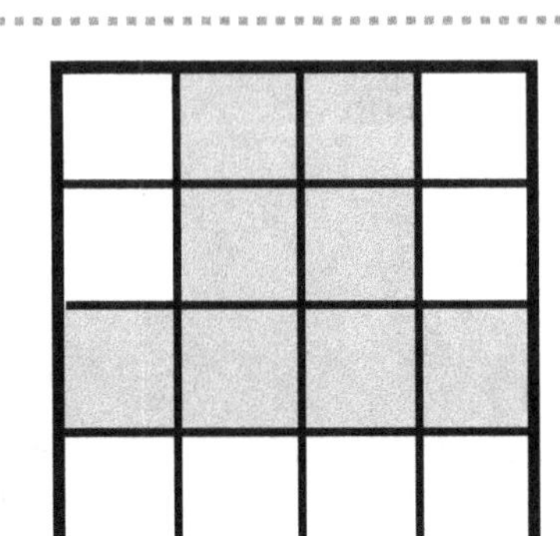

_____ square units

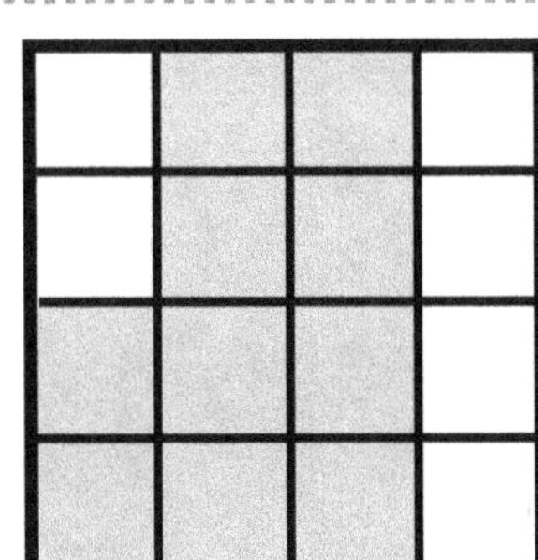

_____ square units

_____ square units

_____ square units

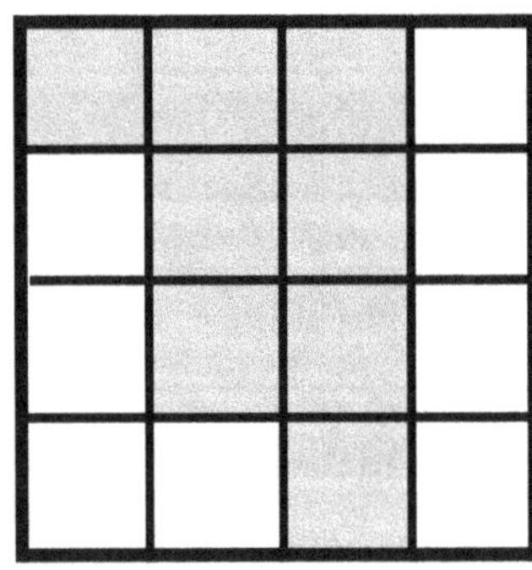

_____ square units

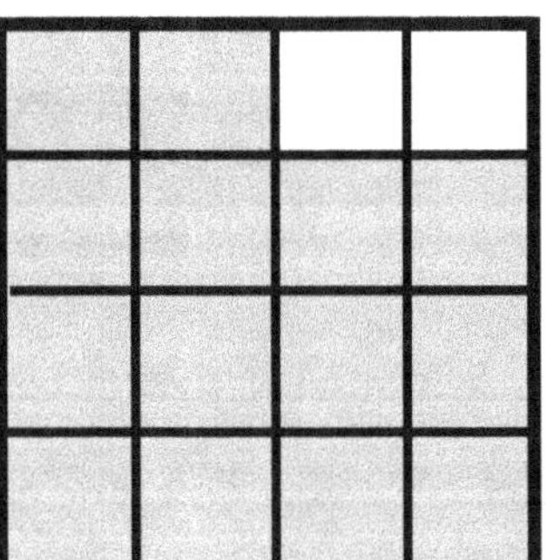

_____ square units

# Exploring Pictographs

Graphs have titles and labels and show information or data.
A pictograph uses pictures to show data.
A key explains the meaning of the picture.

Key  = 1 vote

Ms. Lang's class made a pictograph about favorite ways to eat apples. Answer the questions.

**Favorite Ways to Eat Apples**

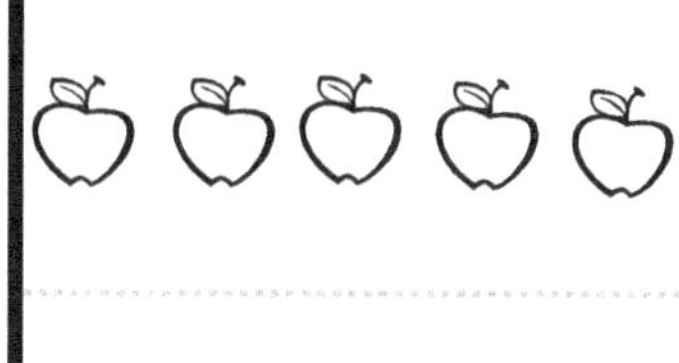

1. What was the least popular way to eat apples? ___________________

2. How many votes were made for apple pie? ___________________

3. How many votes were made in total? ___________________

# Reading Tally Charts

Each tally mark represents 1.
A tally chart counts data in groups of 5.

A group of 5 looks like this.

 = 5

## Answer the questions.

### Favorite Colors

| Color | Tally Marks | Number |
|-------|-------------|--------|
| green | || | |
| red | ||||| | | |
| blue | ||||| |||| | |
| yellow | |||| | |

1. What color was chosen the most?

_______________________________

2. How many people chose red?

_______________________________

3. How many people chose either green or blue?

_______________________________

### Favorite Vegetables

| Vegetable | Tally Marks | Number |
|-----------|-------------|--------|
| carrots | ||||| | |
| cucumbers | ||||| | |
| green beans | ||||| ||| | |
| lettuce | || | |

4. What vegetable was chosen the most?

_______________________________

5. How many more people chose carrots than lettuce?

_______________________________

6. If 3 more people chose carrots, how many people would have chosen carrots in total?

_______________________________

### Favorite Cookies

| Cookie | Tally Marks | Number |
|--------|-------------|--------|
| chocolate chip | || | |
| peanut butter | |||| | |
| double chocolate | ||||| | |

7. How many people chose double chocolate?

_______________________________

8. How many more people chose peanut butter than chocolate chip?

_______________________________

# Exploring Bar Graphs

A bar graph shows data using bars.
The bars can go up or across the graph.
Bar graphs are used to compare information.

Ms. Ng's class made a bar graph about favorite activities at recess.
Answer the questions.

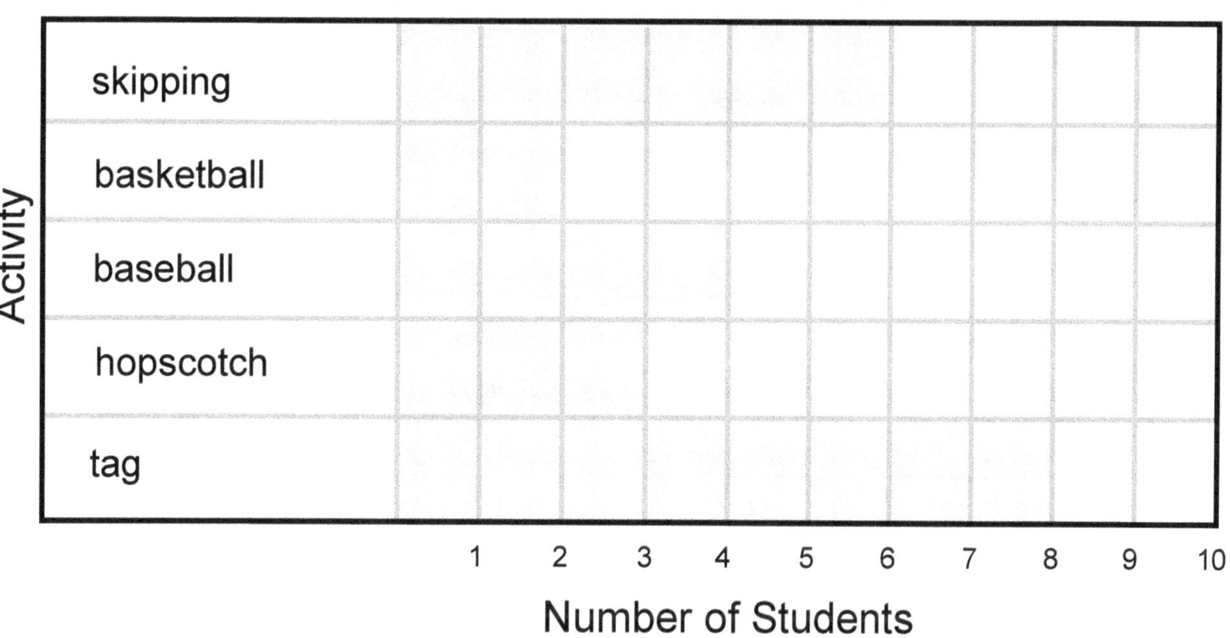



1. The **most** popular recess activity is _______________________

2. The **least** popular recess activity is _______________________

3. How many students liked hopscotch? _______

4. How many more students liked tag over basketball? _______

# Exploring Graphs

Complete the tally chart and bar graph. Answer the questions.

Here are the results of a pet survey.

### Favorite Pets Chart

| Pet | Tally | Number |
|---|---|---|
| Dog | | 4 |
| Cat | | 8 |
| Hamster | | 1 |
| Bird | | 5 |

### Favorite Pets Graph

| Pet | 0 | 1 | 2 | 3 | 4 | 5 | 6 | 7 | 8 | 9 | 10 | 11 |
|---|---|---|---|---|---|---|---|---|---|---|---|---|
| Dog | | | | | | | | | | | | |
| Cat | | | | | | | | | | | | |
| Hamster | | | | | | | | | | | | |
| Bird | | | | | | | | | | | | |

Number of People

1. What was the **most** popular pet? ___________________________________

2. What was the **least** popular pet? ___________________________________

3. How many people chose either a dog or a bird? ___________________

4. How many more people chose a cat than a hamster? ______________

5. How many people chose a hamster? ___________________________

# How Likely Is It?

Certain events always happen.
Impossible events never happen.
Likely events happen often, but not always.
Unlikely events can happen, but not very often.

Answer the questions.

Write **certain**, **impossible**, **likely**, or **unlikely** for each event.

1. I will get up in the morning. _______________________

2. It will snow in July. _______________________

3. It will be hot in summer. _______________________

4. Spring will come after winter. _______________________

5. I will go outside for recess. _______________________

6. I will be younger next year. _______________________

7. I will not brush my teeth for 5 days. _______________________

8. A horse will fly. _______________________

9. The sun will rise tomorrow. _______________________

10. I will grow taller. _______________________

# Exploring Polygons

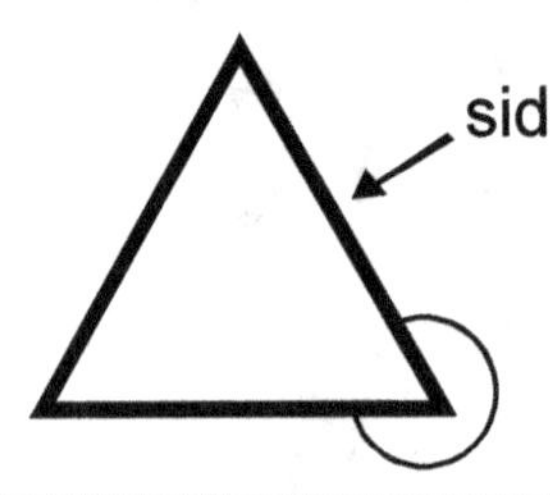


A polygon is a 2D shape with more than 3 sides.

A corner of a polygon is a vertex.
The plural of vertex is vertices.

Fill in the chart.

| Shape | Trace the Shape | Number of Sides | Number of Vertices |
|---|---|---|---|
| triangle | | | |
| square | | | |
| pentagon | | | |
| hexagon | | | |
| octagon | | | |

# Sorting 2D Shapes

Read the rule. Color the shapes that follow the rule.

Shapes with fewer than 5 sides.

Shapes with 4 sides.

Shapes with more than 4 vertices.

Shapes that are polygons.

Shapes with less than 5 vertices.

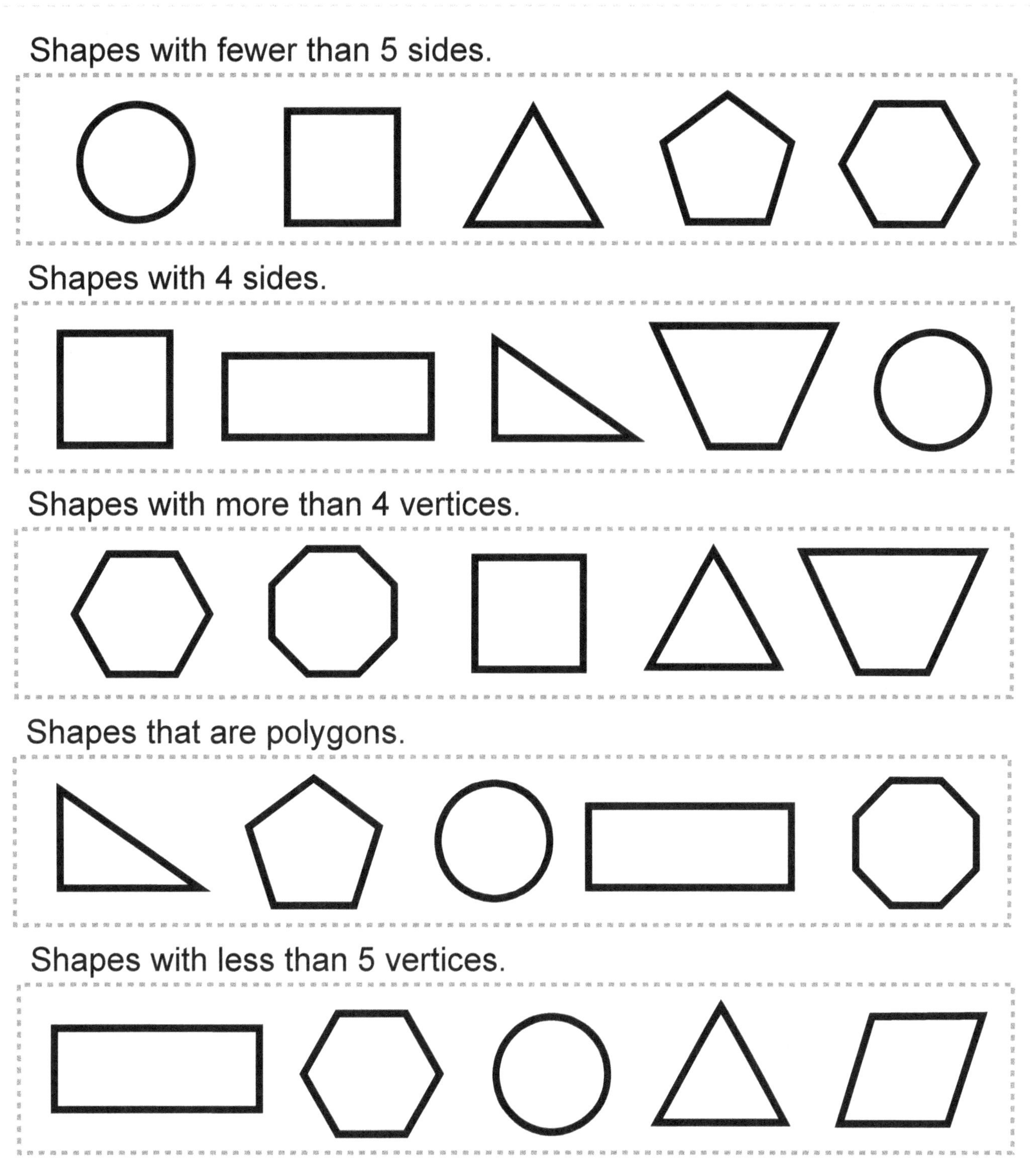

# Identifying 3D Objects

1. Draw a line from the 3D object to its name.

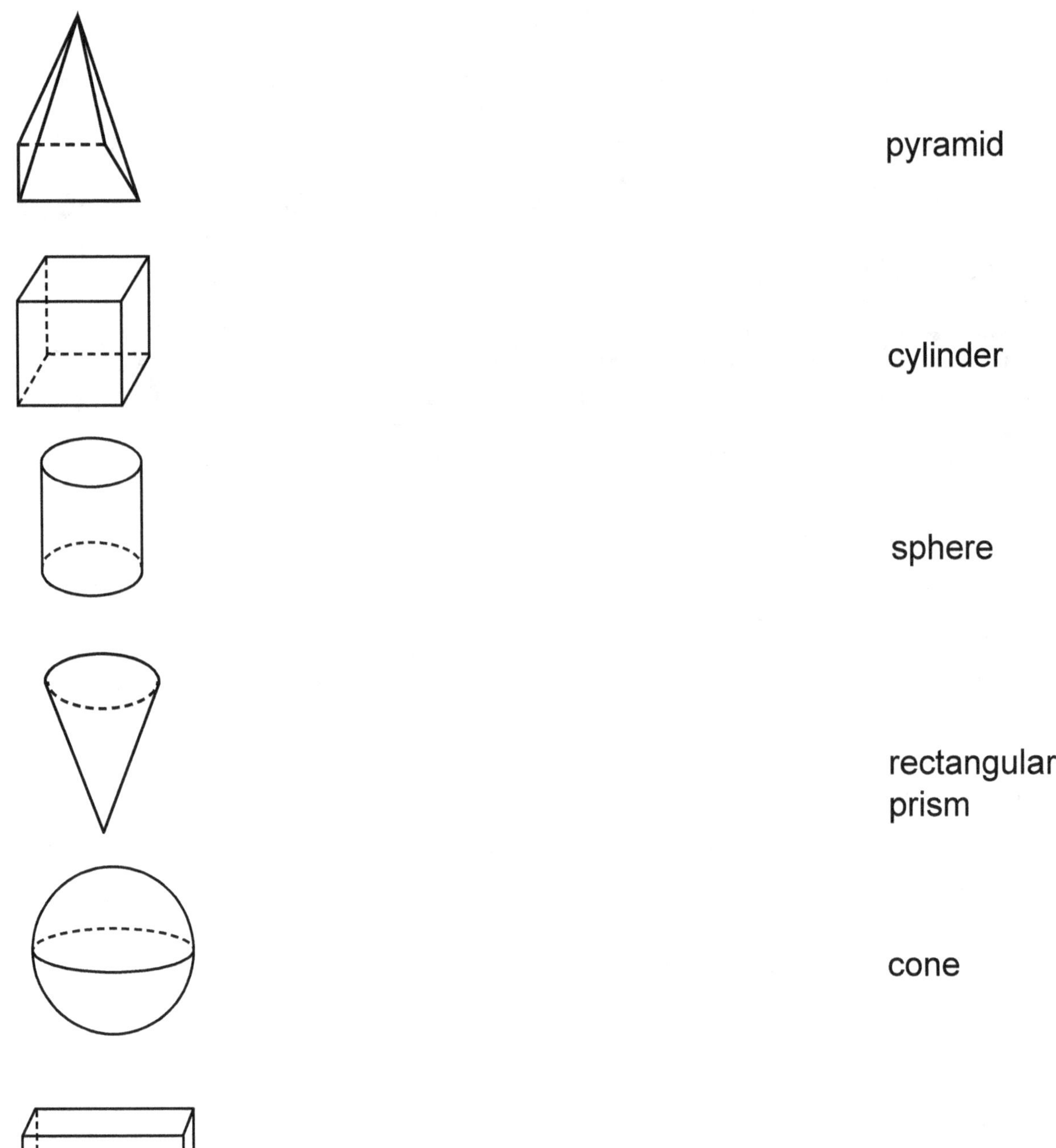

# Identifying 3D Objects (continued)

2. Match the name of the 3D object to an item it looks like.
   Circle the answer.

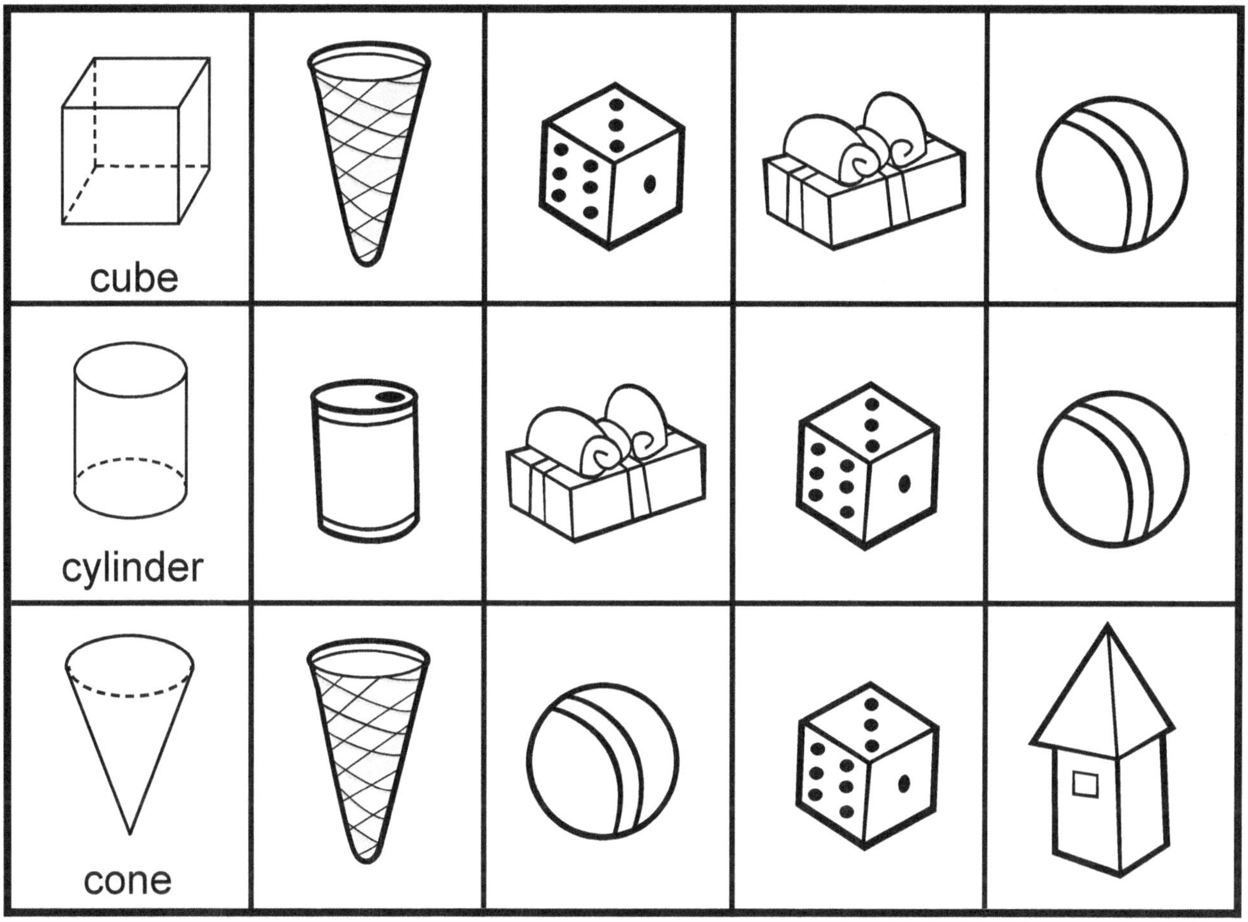

| cube | | | | |
|------|--|--|--|--|
| cylinder | | | | |
| cone | | | | |

## BRAIN STRETCH

1.
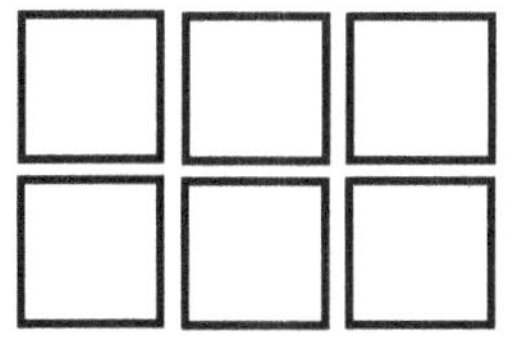

Circle the 3D object that can be made from the pieces.

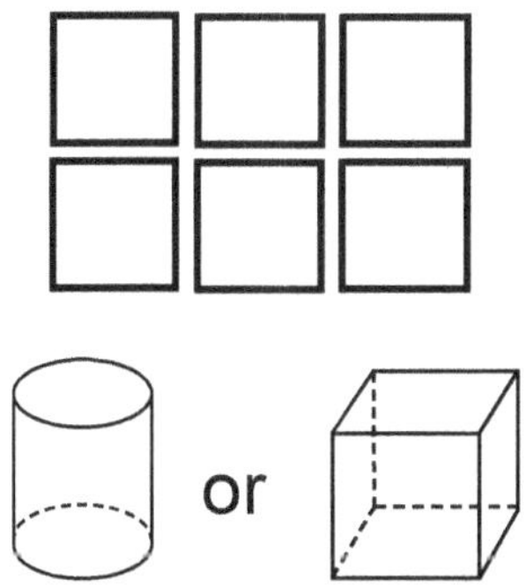

2.
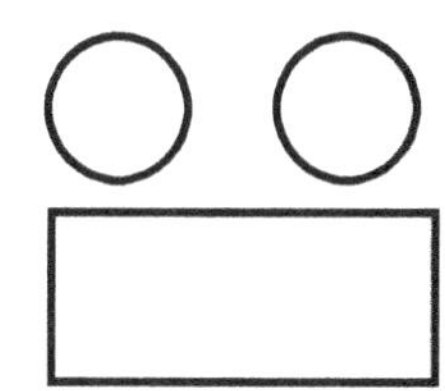
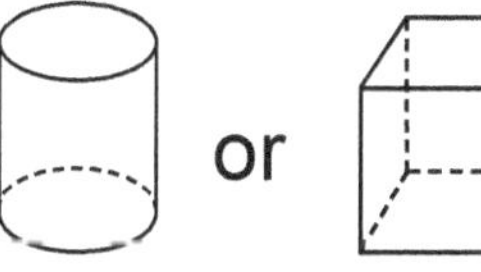

or

or

# Exploring Symmetry

A line of symmetry divides a shape into 2 parts that are the exact same size and shape.

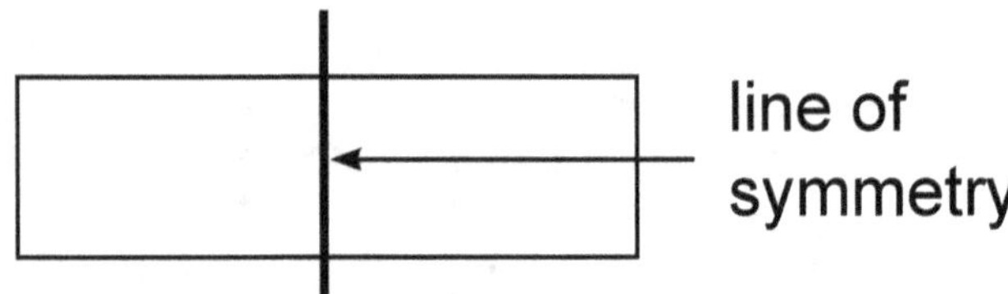



This shape does not have a line of symmetry.

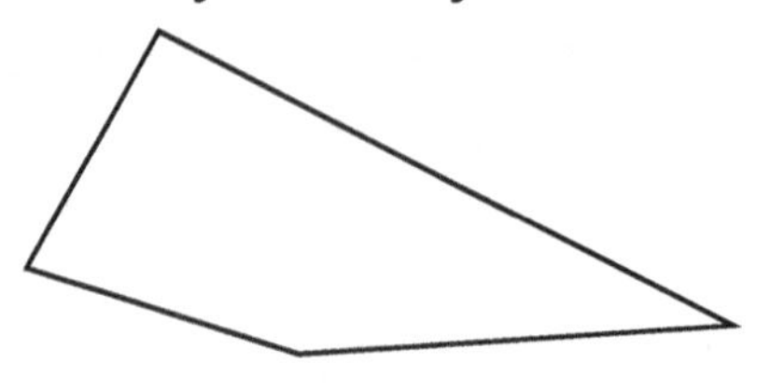

1. Does this show a line of symmetry? Circle the answer.

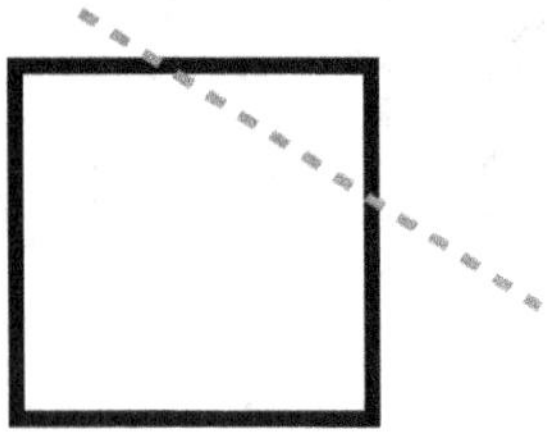

| | | |
|---|---|---|
| Yes    No | Yes    No | Yes    No |
| Yes    No | Yes    No | Yes    No |
| Yes    No | Yes    No | Yes    No |

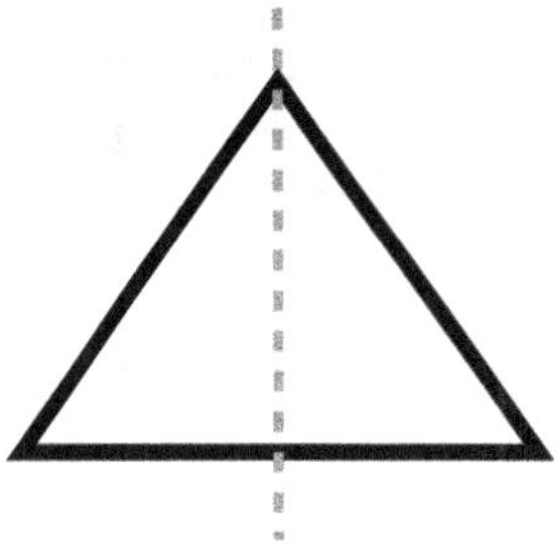

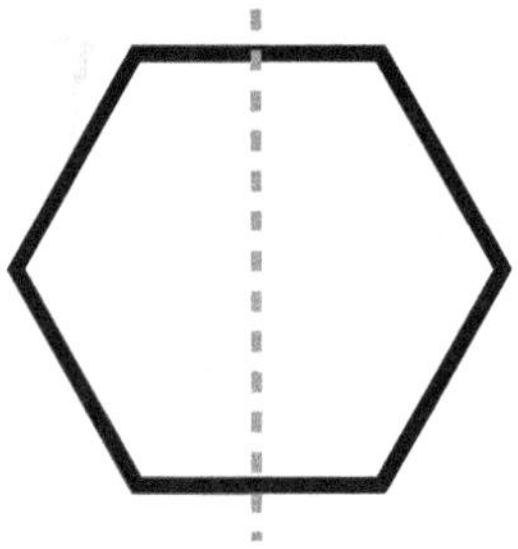

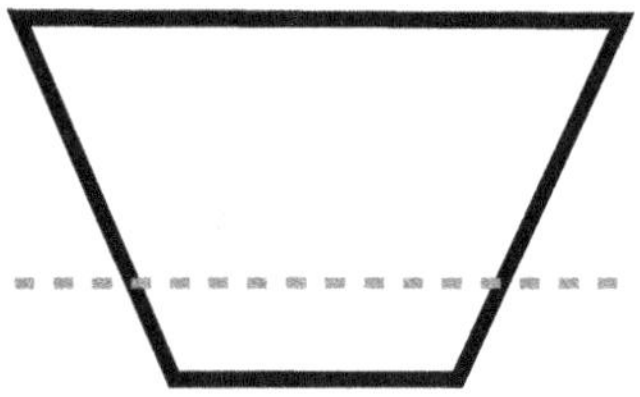

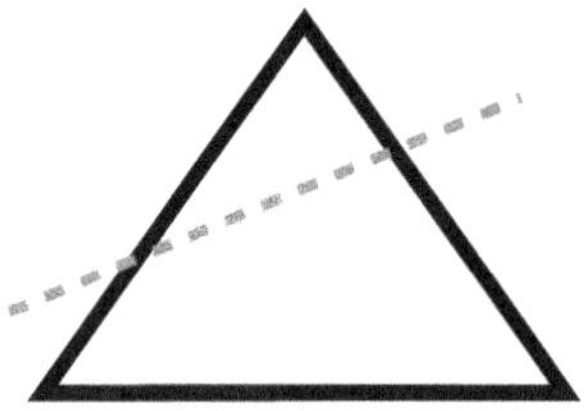

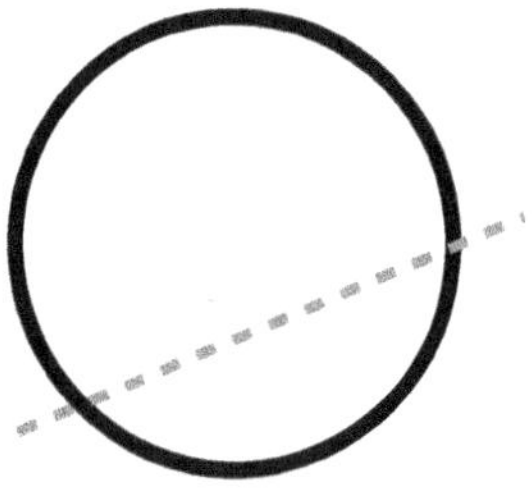

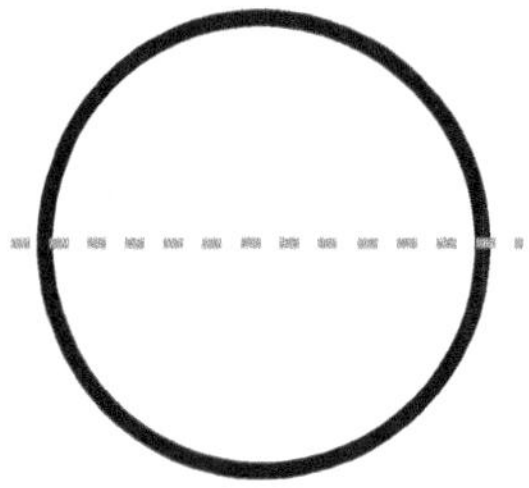

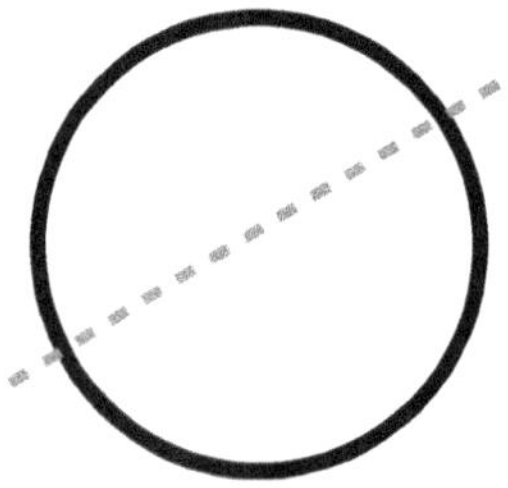

# Exploring Symmetry (continued)

2. Draw the other half of the shape.

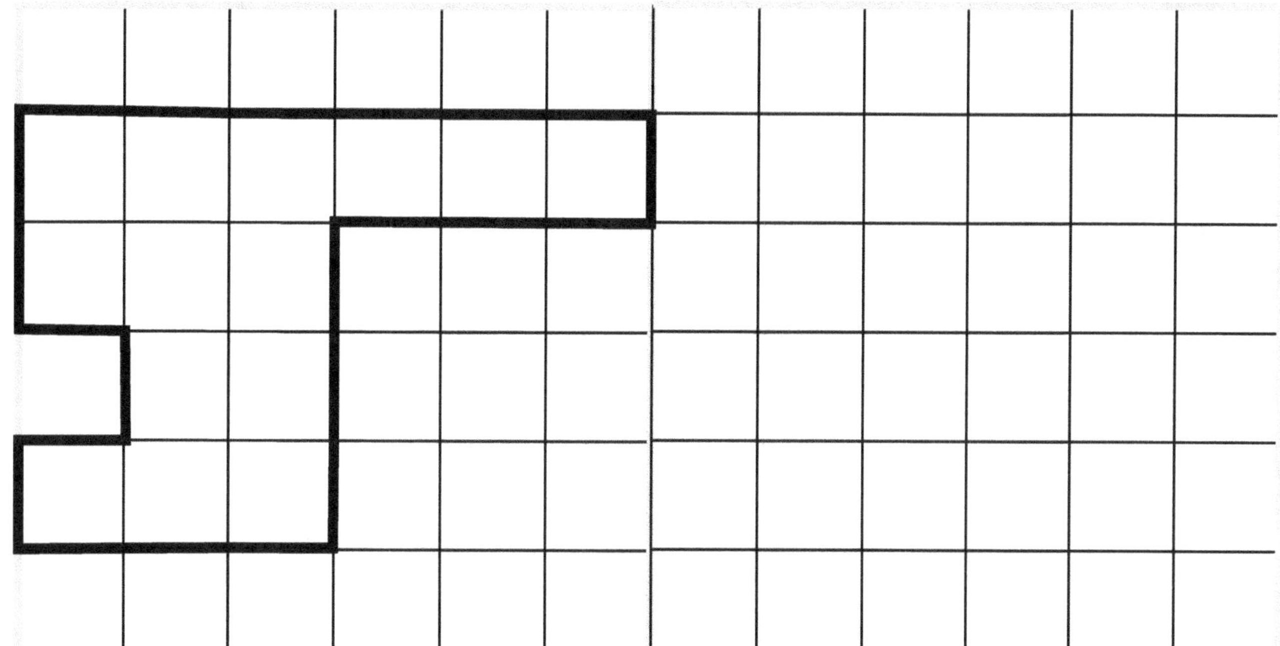

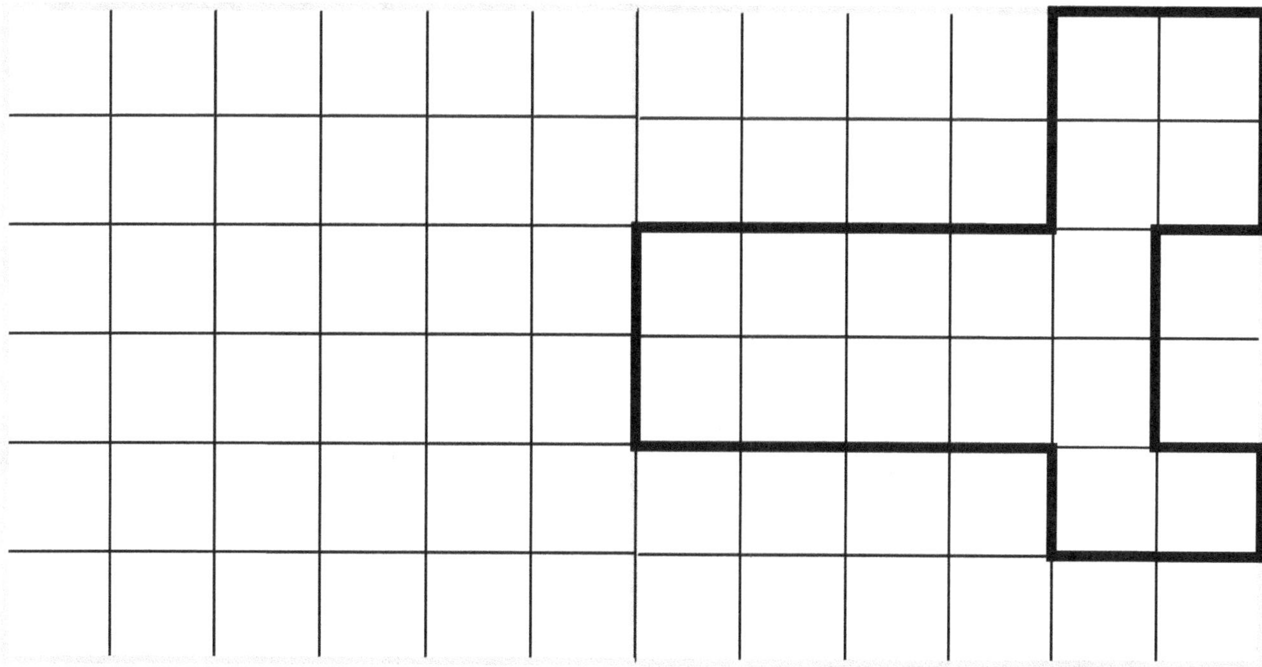

# Following Directions

Read the directions and color the picture.

# Exploring Ordered Pairs

An ordered pair describes a point on a grid. It has numbers in a certain order.
- The first number tells how many units to count to the right.
- The second number tells how many units to count up.

Hint: Always start counting at the bottom left corner, at 0.
Count 1 unit right. Go up 8 units. The ordered pair is (1,8)

Look at the grid of creatures and name the coordinates.

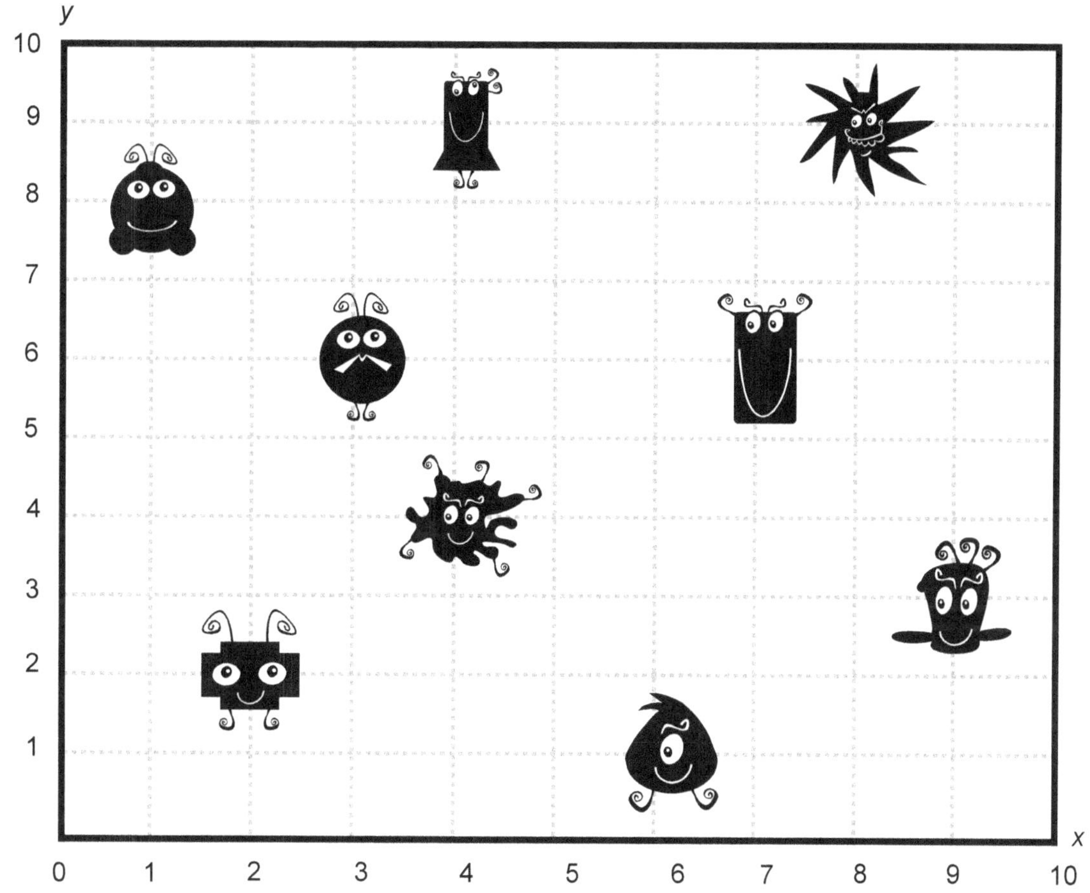

( **1** , **8** )  (   ,   )  (   ,   )  (   ,   )  (   ,   )  (   ,   )

(   ,   )  (   ,   )  (   ,   )

# Incredible Math!

## Answers

**Number Word Search p. 1**

| o | a | s | e | v | e | n | t | e | e | n | n |
|---|---|---|---|---|---|---|---|---|---|---|---|
| n | e | i | g | h | t | e | e | n | b | c | i |
| e | e | n | i | n | e | t | e | e | n | v | n |
| s | i | a | e | l | e | v | e | n | z | a | e |
| e | g | z | t | w | e | l | v | e | z | f | m |
| v | h | g | o | t | o | t | h | e | z | o | o |
| e | t | q | f | i | f | t | e | e | n | q | i |
| n | q | q | t | w | e | n | t | y | a | b | a |
| a | f | o | u | r | t | e | e | n | t | w | o |
| s | i | x | t | e | e | n | t | h | r | e | e |
| s | i | x | t | h | i | r | t | e | e | n | w |
| f | o | u | r | a | f | i | v | e | t | e | n |

**Skip Counting by 2s p. 2**

**1.** 44, 46, 48, 50, 52, 54, 56 **2.** 15, 17, 19, 21, 23, 25, 27 **3.** 82, 84, 86, 88, 90, 92, 94 **4.** 26, 28, 30, 32, 34, 36, 38
**5.** 33, 35, 37, 39, 41, 43, 45 **6.** 50, 52, 54, 56, 58, 60, 62 **7.** 68, 70, 72, 74, 76, 78, 80 **8.** 30, 28, 26, 24, 22, 20, 18
**9.** 48, 46, 44, 42, 40, 38, 36 **10.** 64, 62, 60, 58, 56, 54, 52

**Skip Counting by 5s p. 3**

**1.** 0, 5, 10, 15, 20, 25, 30 **2.** 35, 40, 45, 50, 55, 60, 65 **3.** 70, 75, 80, 85, 90, 95, 100
**4.** 50, 45, 40, 35, 30, 25, 20 **5.** 35, 30, 25, 20, 15, 10, 5 **6.** 70, 65, 60, 55, 50, 45, 40
Brain Stretch: A circle drawn around 5 groups of 5 letters, with a single letter remaining; 26 letters.

**Skip Counting by 10s p. 4**

**1.** 20, 30, 40, 50, 60, 70, 80 **2.** 15, 25, 35, 45, 55, 65, 75 **3.** 22, 32, 42, 52, 62, 72, 82 **4.** 43, 53, 63, 73, 83, 93, 103
**5.** 27, 37, 47, 57, 67, 77, 87 **6.** 100, 90, 80, 70, 60, 50, 40 **7.** 66, 56, 46, 36, 26, 16, 6 **8.** 88, 78, 68, 58, 48, 38, 28

**Skip Counting by 5s to 200 p. 5**

Students connect the dots by 5s from 0 to 200.  Brain Stretch: Count back by 5s: 100, 95, 90, 85, 80, 75, 70, 65
Count back by 2s: 150, 148, 146, 144, 142, 140, 138, 136

**Counting Backward by 1s p. 6**

Students connect the dots by 1 starting at 50.  Brain Stretch: 57, 58, 59, 60, 61, 62; 67, 68, 69

**Growing Number Patterns p. 7**

**1.** 3, 6, 9, 12, 15, 18, 21, 24, 27 **2.** 15, 20, 25, 30, 35, 40, 45, 50, 55 **3.** 5, 15, 25, 35, 45, 55, 65, 75, 85
**4.** Example: 4; 6, 10, 14, 18, 22, 26, 30, 34, 38

**Shrinking Number Patterns p. 8**

**1.** 27, 24, 21, 18, 15, 12, 9, 6 **2.** 35, 30, 25, 20, 15, 10, 5, 0 **3.** 100, 90, 80, 70, 60, 50, 40, 30
**4.** Example: 2; 25, 23, 21, 19, 17, 15, 13, 11

**Odd and Even Numbers p. 9**

Check that students color the picture correctly.


**Ordering Numbers p. 10**

**1.** <u>64</u>, 65, 66; 11, 12, <u>13</u>; <u>88</u>, 89, <u>90</u>; 4, <u>5</u>, 6; 16, 17, <u>18</u>; 69, <u>70</u>, 71; <u>39</u>, 40, <u>41</u>; 33, 34, <u>35</u>; <u>55</u>, 56, 57

**2.** 11, 18, 27, 29, 54, 71; 3, 17, 39, 40, 63, 84 **3.** 71, 46, 24; 19, 15, 11


**Tens and Ones pp. 11–12**

**1.** <u>2</u> tens + <u>8</u> ones; 28 **2.** <u>4</u> tens + <u>5</u> ones; 45 **3.** 1 ten + <u>9</u> ones; 19 **4.** <u>2</u> tens + <u>6</u> ones; 26 **5.** <u>1</u> ten + <u>7</u> ones; 17

**6.** <u>3</u> tens + <u>0</u> ones; 30 **7.** <u>2</u> tens + <u>3</u> ones; 23 **8.** <u>7</u> tens + <u>0</u> ones; 70 **9.** <u>4</u> tens + <u>2</u> one; 42 **10.** <u>4</u> tens + <u>4</u> ones; 44

**11.** <u>8</u> tens + <u>0</u> ones; 80 **12.** <u>3</u> tens + 1 ones; 31 **13.** <u>2</u> tens + <u>2</u> ones; 22 **14.** <u>6</u> tens + <u>2</u> ones; 62 **15.** <u>1</u> tens + 5 ones; 15

**16.** <u>0</u> tens + <u>4</u> ones; 4 **17.** <u>4</u> tens + <u>9</u> ones; 49 **18.** <u>8</u> tens + 5 ones; 85 Brain Stretch: 49; 28; 89; 75


**Writing Numbers in Different Ways p. 13**

**1.** 40 + 1; 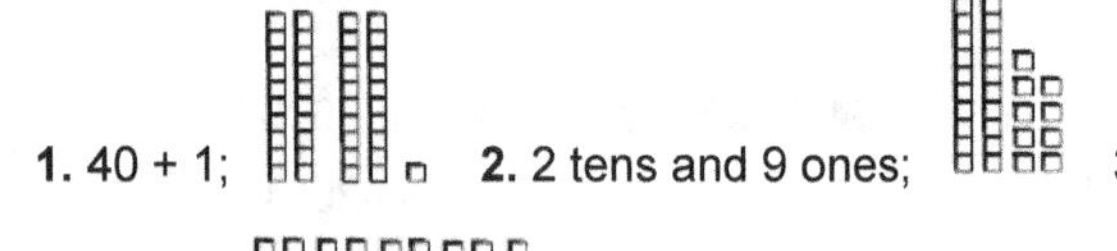 **2.** 2 tens and 9 ones; 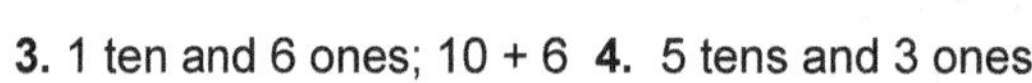 **3.** 1 ten and 6 ones; 10 + 6 **4.** 5 tens and 3 ones; 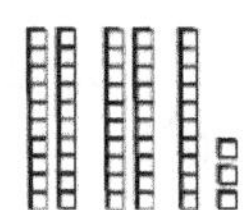

**5.** 90 + 0;


**Writing Numbers in Standard Form p. 14**

**1.** 45 **2.** 76 **3.** 19 **4.** 62 **5.** 84 **6.** 11 **7.** 56 **8.** 8 **9.** 53 **10.** 4 **11.** 39 **12.** 83


**Sum Fun p. 15**

**1.** Check that students color the picture correctly. **2.** 5 + 4 = 9; 6 + 6 = 12; 3 + 6 = 9; 1 + 7 = 8; 0 + 1 = 1; 9 + 5 = 14; 4 + 2 = 6; 2 + 2 = 4; 7 + 7 = 14; 7 + 3 = 10; 4 + 1 = 5; 2 + 1 = 3; 5 + 2 = 7; 5 + 3 = 8; 9 + 2 = 11; 10 + 10 = 20; 8 + 2 = 10; 9 + 9 = 18


**Adding 1 or 2 by Counting On pp. 16–17**

**1.** 13, 12, <u>13</u>; 9, 7, <u>8</u>, <u>9</u>; 24, 23, <u>24</u>; <u>32</u>, 30, <u>31</u>, <u>32</u>; 42, 41, <u>42</u>; 90, 88, <u>89</u>, <u>90</u> **2.** 30, 29, <u>30</u>; 35, 33, <u>34</u>, <u>35</u>; 47, 46, <u>47</u>; 56, 54, <u>55</u>, <u>56</u>; 20, 19, <u>20</u>; 83, 81, <u>82</u>, <u>83</u>; 10, 9, <u>10</u>; 27, 25, <u>26</u>, <u>27</u>; 39, 38, <u>39</u>; 2, 0, <u>1</u>, <u>2</u>; 18, 17, <u>18</u>; 15, 13, <u>14</u>, <u>15</u>


**Addition Doubles p. 18**

**1.** 2 + 2 = 4; **2.** 5 + 5 = 10; **3.** 1 + 1 = 2; **4.** 3 + 3 = 6; **5.** 6 + 6 = 12; **6.** 4 + 4 = 8


**Addition Doubles Plus 1 p. 19**

20, 21; 6, 7; 10, 11; 16, 17; 2, 3; 18, 19; 4, 5; 8, 9; 14, 15


**Numbers Can Be Added in Any Order pp. 20–21**

**1.** 7 + 3 = <u>10</u>, 3 + 7 = <u>10</u>, one 10-frame shows 7 + 3 and the other one shows 3 + 7; 6 + 4 = <u>10</u>, 4 + 6 = <u>10</u>, one 10-frame shows 6 + 4 and the other one shows 4 + 6; 1 + 9 = <u>10</u>, 9 + 1 = <u>10</u>, one 10-frame shows 1 + 9 and the other one shows 9 + 1; 3 + 5 = <u>8</u>, 5 + 3 = <u>8</u>, one 10-frame shows 3 + 5 and the other one shows 5 + 3; 2 + 8 = <u>10</u>, 8 + 2 = <u>10</u>, one 10-frame shows 8 + 2 and the other one shows 2 + 8 **2.** 1 + 4 = <u>5</u>, 4 + 1 = <u>5</u>, one 10-frame shows 1 + 4 and the other one shows 4 + 1; 7 + 2 = <u>9</u>, 2 + 7 = <u>9</u>, one 10-frame shows 7 + 2 and the other one shows 2 + 7; 4 + 3 = <u>7</u>, 3 + 4 = <u>7</u>, one 10-frame shows 4 + 3 and the other one shows 3 + 4; 1 + 8 = <u>9</u>, 8 + 1 = <u>9</u>, one 10-frame shows 1 + 8 and the other one shows 8 + 1; 2 + 1 = <u>3</u>, 1 + 2 = <u>3</u>, one 10-frame shows 2 + 1 and the other one shows 1 + 2; Sample question: 0 + 8 = <u>8</u>, 8 + 0= <u>8</u>, one 10-frame shows 0 + 8 and the other one shows 8 + 0

**Using a Number Line to Add pp. 22–23**
Note: Students may show the dot at either addend (commutative property).
**1.** 9 + 7 = <u>16</u>, a number line showing a dot at 9 and 7 steps from 9 to 16; 6 + 12 = <u>18</u>, a number line showing a dot at 12 and 6 steps from 12 to 18; 11 +4 = <u>15</u>, a number line showing a dot at 11 and 4 steps from 11 to 15; 2 + 15 = <u>17</u>, a number line showing a dot at 15 and 2 steps from 15 to 17.  **2.** 21 + 2 = <u>23</u>, a number line showing a dot at 21 and 2 steps from 21 to 23; 24 + 5 = <u>29</u>, a number line showing a dot at 24 and 5 steps from 24 to 29; 32 + 4 = <u>36</u>, a number line showing a dot at 32 and steps from 32 to 36; 46 + 6 = <u>52</u>, a number line showing a dot at 46 and 6 steps from 46 to 52; 70 + 7 = <u>77</u>, a number line showing a dot at 70 and 7 steps from 70 to 77; 63 + 3 = <u>66</u>, a number line showing a dot at 63 and 3 steps from 63 to 66; 49 + 1 = <u>50</u>, a number line showing a dot at 49 and 1 step from 49 to 50

**Making 10 to Add p. 24**
For each question, there should be a group of 10 circled. 6 + 9 = 10 + <u>5</u> = <u>15</u>; 8 + 8 = 10 + 6 = <u>16</u>; 7 + 5 = 10 + <u>2</u> = <u>12</u>; 14 + 4 = 10 + 8 = <u>18</u>; 9 + 9 = 10 + 8 = <u>18</u>

**Making Addition Sentences pp. 25–26**
Look for 3 addition sentences and blocks colored correctly to represent each sum. Examples:
**1.** 2 + 6 = 8, 4 + 4 = 8, 5 + 3 = 8; 10 + 1 = 11, 9 + 2 = 11, 3 + 8 = 11; 1 + 8 = 9, 2 + 7 = 9, 3 + 6 = 9;  12 + 1 = 13, 10 + 3 = 13, 9 + 4 = 13 **2.** 4 + 8 = 12, 5 + 7 = 12, 6 + 6 = 12; 1 + 5 = 6, 2 + 4 = 6, 3 + 3 = 6; 2 + 8 = 10, 3 + 7 = 10, 4 + 6 = 10; 12 + 2 = 14, 13 + 1 = 14, 10 + 4 = 14

**Addition Practice p. 27**
8 + 6 = <u>14</u>; 7 + 7 = <u>14</u>; 12 + 3 = <u>15</u>; 6 + 6 = <u>12</u>; 15 + 3 = <u>18</u>; 17 + 2 = <u>19</u>; 11 + 0 = <u>11</u>; 10 + 3 = <u>13</u>; 11 + 7 = <u>18</u>; 4 + 9 = <u>13</u>; 8 + 10 = <u>18</u>; 9 + 8 = <u>17</u>; 13 + 1 = <u>14</u>; 13 + 4 = <u>17</u>; 14 + 3 = <u>17</u>; 9 + 5 = <u>14</u>; 11 + 7 = <u>18</u>; 9 + 9 = <u>18</u>; 5 + 13 = <u>18</u>; 3 +12 = <u>15</u>

**Missing Numbers p. 28**
3 + <u>3</u> = 6, 9 + <u>9</u> = 18, 3 + <u>9</u> = 12, <u>8</u> + 6 = 14, 4 + <u>11</u> = 15, 9 + <u>8</u> = 17, <u>9</u> + 2 = 11, 7 + <u>5</u> = 12, <u>6</u> + 7 = 13,  6 + <u>6</u> = 12, 3 + 2 = 5, 7 + <u>0</u> = 7, <u>8</u> + 10 = 18, <u>5</u> + 9= 14, 1 + <u>10</u> = 11, <u>8</u> + 8 = 16, 10 + <u>10</u> = 20, <u>6</u> + 4 = 10, 2 + <u>4</u> = 6, 10 + <u>5</u> = 15

**Addition Riddle p. 29**
12 = A; 20 = B; 9 = C; 10 = D; 6 = E; 4 = G; 11 = H; 18 = I; 15 = L; 13 = N; 17 = R; 16 = S; 7 = T; 8 = U; 14 = W; 3 = Y; riddle: because her students were really bright

**Addition Word Problems p. 30**
**1.** 6 + 2 = 8; 8 **2.** 8 + 7 = 15; 15 **3.** 12 + 2 = 14; 14 **4.** 13 + 3 = 16; 16

**Subtracting 1 or 2 by Counting Back pp. 31–32**
**1.** 7; 8, <u>7</u>; 7, 9, <u>8</u>, <u>7</u>; 16, 17, <u>16</u>; 12, 14, <u>13</u>, <u>12</u>; 14, 15, <u>14</u>; 14, 16, <u>15</u>, <u>14</u>; 12, 13, <u>12</u>; 17, 19, <u>18</u>, <u>17</u>
**2.** 17, 18, <u>17</u>; 9, 11, <u>10</u>, <u>9</u>; 28, 29, <u>28</u>; 18, 20, <u>19</u>, <u>18</u>; 11, 12, <u>11</u>; 31, 33, <u>32</u>, <u>31</u>; 43, 44, <u>43</u>; 23, 25, <u>24</u>, <u>23</u>; 65, 66, <u>65</u>; 56, 58, <u>57</u>, <u>56</u>; 51, 52, <u>51</u>; 40, 42, <u>41</u>, <u>40</u>; 60, 61, <u>60</u>; 85, 87, <u>86</u>, <u>85</u>

**Subtraction Fun p. 33**
**1.** Check that students color the picture correctly.  **2.** 10 − 4 = 6; 3 − 0 = 3; 14 − 5 = 9; 8 − 5 = 3; 15 − 7 = 8; 17 − 9 = 8; 6 − 3 = 3; 9 − 2 = 7; 12 − 6 = 6; 2 − 1 = 1; 16 − 8 = 8; 7 − 1 = 6; 13 − 7 = 6; 5 − 4 = 1; 18 − 9 = 9; 10 − 10 = 0; 11 − 3 = 8; 4 − 1 = 3

**Using a Number Line to Subtract pp. 34–35**
**1.** 19 − 6 = <u>13</u>, a number line showing a dot at 19 and 6 steps back from 19 to 13; 16 − 3 = <u>13</u>, a number line showing a dot at 16 and 3 steps back from 16 to 13; 14 − 4 = <u>10</u>, a number line showing a dot at 14 and 4 steps back from 14 to 10; 17 − 1 = <u>16</u>, a number line showing a dot at 17 and 1 step back from 17 to 16.  **2.** 24 − 2 = <u>22</u>, a number line showing a dot at 24 and 2 steps back from 24 to 22; 33 − 3 = <u>30</u>, a number line showing a dot at 33 and 3 steps back from 33 to 30; 46 − 3 = <u>43</u>, a number line showing a dot at 46 and 3 steps back from 46 to 43; 55 − 4 = <u>51</u>, a number line showing a dot at 55 and 4 steps back from 55 to 51; 22 − 5 = <u>17</u>, a number line showing a dot at 22 and 5 steps back from 22 to 17; 31 − 7 = <u>24</u>, a number line showing a dot at 31 and 7 steps back from 31 to 24; 62 − 8 = <u>54</u>, a number line showing a dot at 62 and 8 steps back from 62 to 54

**Making Subtraction Sentences pp. 36–37**
**1.** Look for 3 subtraction sentences and blocks colored correctly to represent each subtraction. Examples: 4 − 3 = 1 (3 blocks crossed out and 1 block colored), 4 − 2 = 2 (2 blocks crossed out and 2 blocks colored), 4 − 0 = 4 (0 blocks crossed out and 4 blocks colored); 6 − 4 = 2 (4 blocks crossed out and 2 blocks colored), 6 − 5 = 1 (5 blocks crossed out and 1 block colored), 6 − 3 = 3 (3 blocks crossed out and 3 blocks colored); 9 − 4 = 5 (4 blocks crossed out and 5 blocks colored), 9 − 5 = 4 (5 blocks crossed out and 4 blocks colored), 9 − 7 = 2 (7 blocks crossed out and 2 blocks colored); 10 − 4 = 6 (4 blocks crossed out and 6 blocks colored), 10 − 5 = 5 (5 blocks crossed out and 5 blocks colored), 10 − 7 = 3 (7 blocks crossed out and 3 blocks colored)  **2.** 8 − 4 = 4 (4 blocks crossed out and 4 blocks colored), 8 − 5 = 3 (5 blocks crossed out and 3 blocks

colored), 8 – 7 = 1 (7 blocks crossed out and 1 block colored); 5 – 4 = 1 (4 blocks crossed out and 1 blocks colored), 5 – 2 = 3 (2 blocks crossed out and 3 blocks colored), 5 – 3= 2 (3 blocks crossed out and 2 blocks colored); 12 – 4 = 8 (4 blocks crossed out and 8 blocks colored), 12 – 5 = 7 (5 blocks crossed out and 7 blocks colored), 12 – 7 = 5 (7 blocks crossed out and 5 blocks colored); 7 – 4 = 3 (4 blocks crossed out and 3 blocks colored), 7 – 5 = 2 (5 blocks crossed out and 2 blocks colored), 7 – 7 = 0 (7 blocks crossed out and 0 blocks colored)

**Subtraction Practice pp. 38–39**
**1.** 7 – 3 = 4; 6 – 2 = 4; 5 – 5 = 0; 4 – 0 = 4; 8 – 3 = 5; 14 – 1 = 13; 11 – 3 = 8; 14 – 8 = 6; 16 – 9 = 7; 10 – 2 = 8; 15 – 6 = 9; 7 – 0 = 7; 18 – 8 = 10; 13 – 6 = 7; 5 – 4 = 1; 12 – 6 = 6; 8– 2 = 6; 16 – 8 = 8; 9 – 2 = 7; 11 – 9 = 2
**2.** 13 – 7 = 6; 12 – 8 = 4; 2 – 1 = 1; 8 – 0= 8; 11 – 4 = 7; 17 – 10 = 7; 9 – 3 = 6; 16 – 2 = 14; 18 – 9 = 9; 10 – 10 = 0; 9 – 4 = 5; 11 – 8 = 3; 6 – 3 = 3; 15 – 7 = 8; 10 – 9 = 1; 4 – 3 = 1; 11 – 2 = 9; 3 – 2 = 1; 16 – 10 = 6; 7 – 7 = 0 Brain Stretch: 12 – 4 – 3 = 5; 18 – 9 – 5 = 4; 14 – 8 – 2 = 4, 17 – 2 – 6 = 9

**Missing Numbers p. 40**
7 – 2 = 5, 1 – 0 = 1, 5 – 3 = 2, 15 – 7 = 8, 9 – 3 = 6, 13 – 9 = 4, 17 – 8 = 9, 20 – 10 = 10, 15 – 9 = 6, 8 – 3 = 5, 17 – 10 = 7, 3 – 1 = 2, 14 – 4 = 10, 12 – 6 = 6, 10 – 5 = 5.

**Subtraction Riddle p. 41**
6 = A; 3 = B; 2 = I; 5 = N; 4 = O; 8 = R; 1 = W; riddle: a rainbow Brain Stretch: a line drawn between each of the following: sixteen and 16; twelve and 12; nineteen and 19

**Subtraction Word Problems p. 42**
**1.** 7 – 2 = 5; 5 **2.** 10 – 3 = 7; 7 **3.** 12 – 3 = 9; 9 **4.** 15 – 5 = 10; 10

**Word Problems p. 43**
**1.** 11 – 5 = 6 **2.** 12 – 8 = 4 **3.** 6 + 9 = 15 **4.** 18 – 8 = 10 **5.** 12 – 5 = 7 **6.** 3 + 7 = 10 **7.** 14 – 4 = 10

**Adding or Subtracting p. 44**
26 + 3 = 29; 17 + 2 = 19; 16 – 5 = 11; 27 – 5 = 22; 18 + 9 = 27; 18 + 2 = 20; 16 – 3 = 13; 29 – 8 = 21; 22 + 6 = 28; 16 + 5 = 21; 30 – 5 = 25; 19 – 1 = 18; 18 + 7 = 25; 15 + 7 = 22; 11 – 4 = 7; 28 – 9 = 19; 2 + 25 = 27; 13 – 7 = 6

**Ordinal Numbers to 10 p. 45**
**1.** 2nd, 3rd, 4th, 5th, 6th, 7th, 8th, 9th, 10th **2.** the first 4 blocks circled, the 7th block crossed out, the 6th block colored
**3.** bee; horse; cat Brain Stretch: the 2nd bird crossed out, the 4th bird circled

**Adding Tens and Ones p. 46**
3 tens and 9 ones, 39; 2 tens and 3 ones, 23; 4 tens and 6 ones, 46; 5 tens and 9 ones, 59

**Taking Apart to Make 10 pp. 47–48**
**1.** 8 + 6 = 10 + 4 = 14 **2.** a model showing 7 black blocks and 8 white blocks, 7 + 8 = 10 + 5 = 15; a model showing 6 black blocks and 9 white blocks. 6 + 9 = 10 + 5 = 15; a model showing 9 black blocks and 7 white blocks, 9 + 7 = 10 + 6 = 16
**3.** a model showing 4 black blocks and 9 white blocks, 4 + 9 = 10 + 3 = 13; a model showing 8 black blocks and 7 white blocks, 8 + 7 = 10 + 5 = 15; a model showing 3 black blocks and 9 white blocks, 3 + 9 = 10 + 2 = 12; a model showing 8 black blocks and 8 white blocks, 8 + 8 = 10 + 6 = 16; a model showing 5 black blocks and 7 white blocks, 5 + 7 = 10 + 2 = 12

**Two-Digit Addition Without Regrouping pp. 49–50**
**1.** first row: 85, 37, 98, 97, 74; second row: 62, 88, 85, 95, 46; third row: 87, 57, 64, 99, 44; fourth row:  97, 52, 48, 33, 95;
**2.** first row: 97, 56, 48, 53, 99; second row: 85, 48, 98, 76, 77; third row: 63, 88, 76, 99, 49; fourth row: 78, 54, 66, 79, 48; fifth row: 97, 56, 58, 66, 98

**Addition Riddle p. 51**
97 = I, 42 = R, 78 = W, 92 = L, 25 = H, 85 = T, 73 = V, 65 = U, 32 = G, 71 = X, 84 = E, 74 = O, 66 = A, 96 = B, 59 = S, 53 = N, He was learning a new language!

**Two-Digit Addition with Regrouping pp. 52–53**
**1.** first row: 82, 41, 92, 61, 82; second row: 70, 90, 81, 62, 72; third row: 71, 61, 50, 100, 44 **2.** first row: 72, 97, 80, 71, 54; second row: 94, 50, 72, 91, 86; third row: 66, 65, 53, 70, 81; fourth row: 82, 65, 73, 91, 54

**Two-Digit Subtraction Without Regrouping pp. 54–55**
**1.** first row: 47, 44, 16, 44, 21; second row: 55, 64, 12, 44, 71; third row: 22, 26, 10, 11, 20; fourth row: 55, 2, 75, 51, 3
**2.** first row: 12, 27, 13, 11, 24; second row: 57, 1, 73, 42, 25; third row: 45, 34, 14, 13, 16; fourth row: 52, 64, 10, 15, 63
Brain Stretch: a model showing 38 –23 = 15; 3 tens blocks and 8 ones blocks – 2 tens blocks and 3 ones blocks = 1 ten block and 5 ones blocks

**Subtraction Match p. 56**
A line drawn from the following questions and answers: 45 – 31 and 14; 96 – 52 and 44; 97 – 30 and 67; 28 – 12 and 16; 73 – 22 and 51; 38 – 35 and 3; 79 – 48 and 31; 84 – 62 and 22

**Making an Easier Problem pp. 57–58**
**1.** 16 – 10 = 6; 14 – 10 = 4, add 1; 18 – 10 = 8, add 3; 19 – 10 = 9, add 3; 21 – 10 = 11, add 4; 23 – 10 = 13, add 4; 21 – 10 = 11, add 3 **2.** 35 – 20 = 15; 26 – 20 = 6, add 4; 32 – 20 = 12, add 3; 29 – 20 = 9, add 1; 44 – 20 = 24, add 2; 35 – 20 = 15, add 4; 35 – 20 = 15, add 1

**Two-Digit Subtraction with Regrouping pp. 59–60**
**1.** first row: 36, 57, 37, 9, 7; second row: 17, 27, 17, 36, 19; third row: 8, 57, 17, 58, 11
**2.** first row: 7, 18, 16, 46, 19; second row: 13, 19, 7, 36, 18; third row: 8, 45, 15, 61, 19; fourth row: 36, 47, 27, 9, 15

**Subtraction Riddle p. 61**
7 = E; 29 = H; 25 = I; 44 = M; 38 = N; 13 = O; 12 = P; 69 = S; 47 = T; 58 = U; 16 = W; 5 = Z; riddle: when someone steps on its mouse

**Word Problems p. 62**
**1.** add 62 marbles  **2.** subtract, 18 birds  **3.** subtract, 46  **4.** add, 66 buttons

**Introducing Multiplication pp. 63–64**
**1.** 6 + 6 = <u>12</u>, 2 × 6 = <u>12</u>; 2 + 2 + 2 = <u>6</u>, 3 × 2 = <u>6</u>; 10 + 10 = <u>20</u>, 2 × 10 = <u>20</u>; 3 + 3 + 3 + 3 = <u>12</u>, 4 × 3 = <u>12</u>; 7 + 7 = <u>14</u>, 2 × 7 = <u>14</u>; 8 + 8 = <u>16</u>, 2 × 8 = <u>16</u>  **2.** 5 + 5 + 5 = 15, 3 × 5 = 15; 8 + 8 = 16, 2 × 8 = 16; 7 + 7 = 14, 2 × 7 = 14; 3 + 3 + 3 + 3 + 3 = 15, 3 × 5 = 15; 9 + 9 = 18, 2 × 9 = 18; 4 + 4 + 4 + 4 = 16, 4 × 4 = 16; 5 + 5 + 5 + 5 = 20, 4 × 5 = 20; 10 + 10 = 20, 2 × 10 = 20; 2 + 2 + 2 + 2 + 2 = 10, 2 × 5 = 10

**Skip Counting p. 65**
**1.** 8 groups, 16  **2.** 8 groups, 40  **3.** 5 groups, 50

**Fractions: Equal Parts p. 66**
Each of the following shapes has one half colored. **1.** first and third shapes  **2.** first shape  **3.** second and third shapes  **4.** second shape  **5.** first and third shapes  **6.** third shape

**Exploring Fractions pp. 67–68**
**1.** A circle drawn around the correct fraction:

$$\frac{1}{3}; \frac{1}{3}; \frac{1}{2}; \frac{1}{2}; \frac{1}{4}; \frac{1}{3}; \frac{1}{4}; \frac{1}{3}; \frac{1}{3}; \frac{1}{4}; \frac{1}{4}$$

**2.** $\frac{1}{8}; \frac{1}{2}; \frac{3}{4}; \frac{5}{9}; \frac{8}{9}; \frac{1}{5}; \frac{3}{5}; \frac{1}{2}; \frac{2}{3}; \frac{2}{8}; \frac{2}{6}; \frac{4}{7}; \frac{1}{3}; \frac{4}{6}; \frac{1}{4}; \frac{1}{2}; \frac{7}{8}$

**Coloring Fractions p. 69**
Check that students have correctly colored the shapes.

Brain Stretch:  Examples: $\frac{1}{3}$ of a circle shaded; $\frac{1}{4}$ of a square shaded; $\frac{1}{2}$ of a rectangle shaded

**Fractions as Part of a Group p. 70**
Check that students have correctly colored each group of shapes. first row: 1 shape, 1 shape, 2 shapes; second row: 1 shape, 1 shape, 2 shapes; third row: 3 shapes, 1 shape, 1 shape

**Fraction Problems p. 71**

**1.** $\frac{1}{4}$  **2.** a picture of 4 mailboxes with 3 of them green; $\frac{3}{4}$  **3.** a picture of 3 books with a circle around 2 books; $\frac{2}{3}$

**4.** a picture of 4 carrots with cheese on 2 of them; $\frac{2}{4}$  **5.** a picture of 2 bars with 1 bar circled; $\frac{1}{2}$

**Telling Time to the Hour p. 72**
Check that students color the hour hand blue. 11 o'clock, 11:00; 5 o'clock, 5:00; 2 o'clock, 2:00; 10 o'clock, 10:00; 8 o'clock, 8:00; 4 o'clock, 4:00; 9 o'clock, 9:00

**Telling Time to the Half Hour p. 73**
Check that students color the hour hand blue and the minute hand red. half past 1, 1:30; half past 6, 6:30; half past 2, 2:30; half past 11, 11:30; half past 3, 3:30; half past 7, 7:30; half past 12, 12:30

**Telling Time to Quarter Past the Hour p. 74**
Check that students color the hour hand blue and the minute hand red. quarter past 1, 1:15; quarter past 2, 2:15; quarter past 5, 5:15; quarter past 6, 6:15; quarter past 7, 7:15; quarter past 9, 9:15; quarter past 4, 4:15

**Telling Time to the Quarter Hour p. 75**
Check that students color the hour hand blue and the minute hand red. quarter to 2, 1:45; quarter to 3, 2:45; quarter to 6, 5:45; quarter to 7, 6:45; quarter to 8, 7:45; quarter to 10, 9:45; quarter to 5, 4:45

**What Time Is It? p. 76**
A circle around the correct time: 4:00; 7:30; 8:00; 11:00; 3:00; 3:30; 10:30; 5:00; 12:30; 9:30; 4:30; 2:00

**Showing the Time p. 77**
Check that students draw 2 hands on the clock and color the hour hand blue and the minute hand red.

**Calendar Time p. 78**
**1.** January, February, March, April, May, June, July, August, September, October, November, December **2.** 12

**Reading a Calendar p. 79**
**1.** Thursday **2.** 5 Tuesdays **3.** 4 Saturdays **4.** seven **5.** 30 days **6.** Saturday **7.** Thursday **8.** 4 Fridays

**Getting to Know Coins pp. 80–82**
**1.** A line drawn from the coin to its value: penny, 1¢ nickel, 5¢; dime, 10¢; quarter, 25¢; half dollar, 50¢; dollar, 100¢ **2.** quarter, 25¢; dime, 10¢; penny, 1¢; half dollar, 50¢; nickel, 5¢; dollar, 100¢ **3.** Check that students follow the coloring directions.
Brain Stretch: 10 dimes; 13 nickels; 6 half dollars; 6 dollars; 13 quarters; 3 pennies

**Estimating p. 83**
Dan: Estimate: 50¢; Count: 10, 20, 30, 40, 45

Tessa: Estimate: 60¢; Count: 25, 50, 60, 70, 80

John: Estimate: 50¢; Count: 10, 20, 30, 40, 45

**Counting Dimes and Nickels p. 84**
10, 15, 20, 25, 30; 1, 11, 21, 26; 10, 20, 30, 40; 1, 11, 16, 21, 26, 31

**How Much Money? pp. 85–86**
**1.** Ben: 25, 25, 25, 10, 5; 90¢; Carrie: 10, 5, 5, 1, 5; 26¢; Tanya: 25, 10, 5, 5, 1; 46¢ **2.** Ben **3.** Carrie **4.** Jane: 25, 10, 10, 10, 10; 65¢; Suzanne: 25, 10, 10, 10, 5; 60¢; Omar: 25, 25, 25, 10, 10; 95¢; James: 1, 10, 5, 5, 5; 26¢ **5.** Omar **6.** James

**Trading Coins p. 87**
35¢, a drawing of a quarter and 1 dime; 50¢, a drawing of 2 quarters; 20¢, a drawing of 2 dimes; 60¢, a drawing of 2 quarters and 1 dime; 65¢, a drawing of 2 quarters, 1 dime, and 1 nickel

**Money Match p. 88**
A line drawn from each item to its coin value. from 95 cents to 2 quarters, 4 dimes, and 1 nickel; from $1.00 to a dollar; from 40 cents to 1 quarter, 1 dime, and 1 nickel; 50 cents to 1 quarter, 1 dime, and 3 nickels; 60 cents to 2 quarters and 1 dime

**Missing Coins p. 89**
25¢ + 5¢ = 30¢, a drawing of 1 nickel; 5¢ + 45¢ = 50¢, a drawing of 1 quarter and 2 dimes; 40¢ + 40¢ = 80¢, a drawing of 1 quarter, 1 dime; and 1 nickel; 10¢ + 55¢ = 65¢, a drawing of 2 quarters and 1 nickel; 50¢ + 50¢ = $1.00, a drawing of 2 quarters; 20¢ + 55¢ = 75¢, a drawing of 2 quarters and 1 nickel

**Equal Amounts p. 90**
Drawings may vary. Examples: 35¢—1 quarter and 1 dime, 1 quarter and 2 nickels; 80¢—3 quarters and 1 nickel, 2 quarters and 3 dimes; 50¢—2 quarters, 5 dimes; $1.00—4 quarters, 1 loonie

**Exploring Length pp. 91–93**
**1.** 7 paper clips; 8 paperclips; 4 paper clips; 5 paper clips     **2.** 9 cm; 6 cm; 10 cm; 3 cm
**3.** 4 cm; 7 cm  Brain Stretch: about 7 cubes

**Exploring Mass p. 94**
first row: 10 blocks, 4 blocks, 5 blocks; second row: 6 blocks, 8 blocks, 7 blocks; third row: 13 blocks, 11 blocks; 12 blocks

**Exploring Capacity p. 95**
**1.** pail **2.** bowl **3.** larger container of milk **4.** pail **5.** box of tissues **6.** bottle of soda **7.** bowl **8.** container of milk **9.** box of toys **10.** box of toys

**Exploring Measurement p. 96**
**1.** measuring cup **2.** thermometer **3.** ruler **4.** balance scale **5.** clock **6.** calendar

**Exploring Perimeter p. 97**
4 + 8 + 6 = 18 units; 9 + 2 + 9 + 2 = 22 units; 3 + 4 + 3 + 1 = 11 units; 4 + 4 + 4 + 4 = 16 units

**Exploring Area p. 98**
8 square units; 10 square units;  8 square units; 6 square units; 8 square units; 14 square units

**Exploring Pictographs p. 99**
**1.** apple pie **2.** 7 students **3.** 18 students

**Reading Tally Charts p. 100**
**1.** blue **2.** 5 people **3.** 10 people **4.** green beans **5.** 2 more people **6.** 11 people **7.** 5 people **8.** 2 more people

**Exploring Bar Graphs p. 101**
**1.** most popular: skipping; **2.** least popular: baseball; **3.** hopscotch: 5 people; **4.** tag over basketball: 2 people

**Exploring Bar Graphs p. 102**
**1.** most popular: cat 8; **2.** least popular: hamster 1; **3.** dog 4 or bird 5; **4.** 7 more people chose a cat; **5.** 1 person chose a hamster

**How Likely Is It? p. 103**
**1.** likely **2.** not likely **3.** likely **4.** certain **5.** likely **6.** impossible **7.** unlikely **8.** impossible **9.** certain

**Exploring Polygons p. 104**
triangle: 3 sides, 3 vertices; square: 4 sides, 4 vertices; pentagon: 5 sides, 5 vertices; hexagon: 6 sides, 6 vertices; octagon: 8 sides, 8 vertices

**Sorting 2D Shapes p. 105**
first row: pentagon and hexagon; second row: square, rectangle, and trapezoid; third row: square, triangle and trapezoid; fourth row: pentagon, rectangle, and octagon; fifth row: rectangle, triangle, rhombus and circle

**Identifying 3D Objects pp. 106–107**
**1.** A line drawn from the object to its name, in order: pyramid, cube, cylinder, cone, sphere, and rectangular prism  **2.** cube: die; cylinder: can and paper towel; cone: ice cream cone  Brain Stretch: cube; cylinder

**Exploring Symmetry pp. 108–109**

**1.** first row: 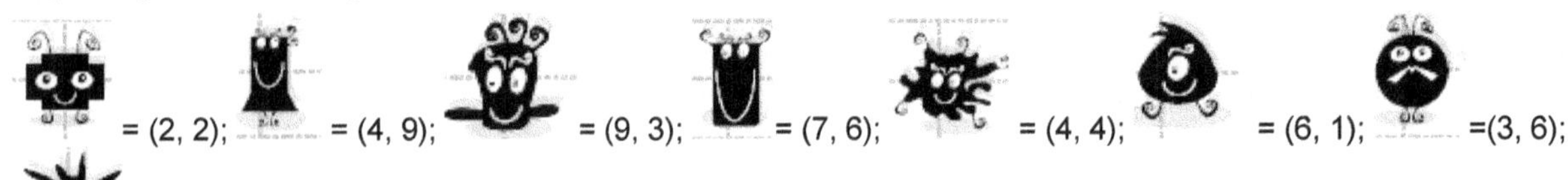 ; second row: ; third row:

2. Students should be able to draw the other half (the horizontal mirror image) of each shape.

**Following Directions p. 110**
Check that students color the picture according to the directions.

**Exploring Coordinates p. 111**

= (2, 2);      = (4, 9);      = (9, 3);      = (7, 6);      = (4, 4);      = (6, 1);      =(3, 6);

= (8, 9)